Yes I Can!

Dr. Izdihar Jamil, Ph.D.

15 Mindset Secrets from Inspiring Entrepreneurs Around the World

Publishing History

Edition 1 / October 2020
ISBN: 9798698869627
Imprint: Independently Published

Dedications

A **big** thank you to my husband, family, and friends for your love and support. Thank you to my best friend who's always cheering for me. Thank you to my coaches and clients for your love and trust. Thank you Mama and Ayah for your love, and I hope I make you proud. To all that have a big vision – this book is for you.

Ba and Nada, Mommy loves you very much!

Kind regards,

~ Dr. Izdihar Jamil

I want to thank Danielle Peralta, my best friend and future wife, for her support and strength as I go through this unbelievable journey.

I also want to thank my parents and brother for their support and unconditional love.

Lastly, I want to thank Dr. Izdihar Jamil for the opportunity to be featured in this powerful book alongside these amazing entrepreneurs.

~ Christian Rey Perez

I am extremely grateful for my family and friends who have supported me as I stepped into this exciting place I have found myself. There have been lots of unknown variables, and your encouragement as I navigate new spaces has been such a gift.

~ Ellie Erickson

I dedicate this book to all the women who go where they want, when they want, or will one day.

~ Gabriele Grikstaite

For the love, support and inspiration that I have generously received from Dr Mohsen El-Labban, my friends, my family, and my husband. This wouldn't have been possible without you.

~ Jess Tayel

I need to take a quick moment and thank my incredible husband, Tyler, for being the man of strength and compassion that he is, and for always believing in me and my dreams. To my many coaches and mentors in my life that have been a support, a sounding board, insisting on accountability, and holding unwavering faith – I am forever grateful!

Thank you!

~ Jessica Fox

Dedications

I want to thank all the powerful, influential women in my life that teach me, hold me accountable, love me and share their knowledge, wisdom and friendship with me. My life would not be what it is without your beautiful gifts bestowed on me daily.

Most of all, I want to thank all my amazing clients… past, present and future. I adore and celebrate each of you.

~ **Linda Buchanan**

First of all, thank you so much, Izdihar, for giving me this opportunity. I would also like to thank my senseis Hanshi Buck, Dana Abbott, Mike Zeleznick, Joe Eagar, and Sean Callagy. I also thank my mother Billie Armstrong and my wife Tiffany Armstrong as well as, and all my family and students for their wisdom, love, and support. I also dedicate this book especially in memory my sister Rose Armstrong and instructors Ron Fugiel and Jason Moore. Your lessons and love are always with me.

~ **Shihan** Michael Armstrong

I dedicate my chapter to all the women who wish to pick up their broken pieces to rebuild themselves from rock bottom to a solid foundation.

~ **Najmunnisa Abdul Kader**

I would like to give thanks to my Almighty Savior, Jesus Christ, my family for believing in me, my friends for showing me support, and all of my role models throughout my life, who taught me to work hard, to never give up, and to stay true to who I am. *#WeSupportThoseWhoSupportUS*

~ **Nate**

I want to thank my husband, Amir Esa, and my son for being with me during those trying moments when I was at my lowest points. Your support, encouragement, and dedication in helping me get back on my feet is greatly appreciated and loved.

~ **Nor Suhir**

Dedications

I dedicate this book to my mom, who raised me with unconditional love. I owe my success to her continuous support. Without her, I wouldn't be the strong, confident woman that I am.

And to my husband, who believes in me like no one ever did. Who showed me that love is action, not a word.

To Sham and Khalid, my amazing kids who spent hours watching over my shoulder as I work.

To my sister, who I shared a lifetime with.

To all my friends who made every day of my life a little better…

Because of you, I laugh a little harder, cry a little less, and smile a lot more.

~ Nour Tarzi

I want to thank my children, Sakeena, Yusef, and Suraya. You have been my inspiration. Thank you for always shining beauty and love into my life.

~ Razia Naqvi-Jukes

I dedicate this book to everyone who had toxic experience with money and to my darling Lily.

~ Tammy Ketura Mock-Andrejowich

To my children: Jaydee, Hyrum, Talon and Quinten.... May you have the courage to follow your dreams.

~ Vandee Flake

Book Reviews

"An Authentic Anthology of stories of women who were courageous to chart their pain to power journey."
~ **Nurazimah Abdul Rahman,** Principal of Maestro Hub Enrichment Center, Singapore

"Najmunnisa's journey of healing to a woman of self-esteem and strength is a truly remarkable read that I would recommend to anyone grappling with self-esteem issues from childhood."
~ **Lisa Marie Pepe,** Confidence Coach and Online Visibility Expert at Positive Transformation Coaching, East Haven, CT, USA

"Reading this international best seller was like having a deep personal chat with some amazing female friends who have gone through challenging and harrowing times in their lives but have now overcome them and are living their lives with a renewed sense of purpose and dedication – the way they see fit. These memoirs are personal. They are raw, and they make you feel. They make you look beyond your own life and appreciate the struggles and challenges of the everyday person who passes you by in the street. They make you question your own adversities, your weaknesses, and your strengths, and you emerge stronger and wiser.

"Najmunnisa's chapter of her life is a truly compelling read. The conversational and laid-back style of her writing shows you that she is real and that her life experience is real. The strength of her writing manages to capture your attention and your admiration, and to quietly reflect on the strength of this inspirational woman who is now a Women's Voice Catalyst."
~ **Mala Desai**, Elementary School Teacher, Canberra, Australian Capital Territory

"Tear-jerking and transformational stories."
~ **Dee Delilah**, Entrepreneur, Kuala Lumpur, Malaysia

"So much inspiration and empowering stories of some amazing life warriors! Truly recommend reading this book!"
~ **Guadalupe Ramirez**, Artist, Heyburn ID, USA

"What an exceptional man that God has chosen to motivate us all through his life story of humble beginnings to successful entrepreneur. Reading his story, you can feel motivation well up inside you. Nate is a role model not just for at-risk youth but for all of us who need a swift kick in the seat of our pants to get up and make our dreams happen!"
~ **Michelle Jensen**, Esq.

"It was like God giving the recipe to a successful cake, and all of his experiences were the ingredients. But just like a cake, it didn't make sense until it went through the fire and came out as Mister Green."
~ **Belinda Kendall**, CEO and Founder, Promise Media Group, LLC and Promise Gospel Network, LLC

"After reading Nate Green, Sr.'s chapter on his life, I notice he has a very similar story to mine. His explanation of starting from the bottom and ending up on top and how he arrived there is inspiring, and every young man should read and learn from it!"
~ **Phil Chalmers**, *Where the Bodies Are Buried* Podcast

"I enjoyed reading your chapter. What I enjoyed most is your vulnerability. So often, we tend to try and hide our story and how it made us feel. You showed raw emotion and that's inspiring. Thank you for sharing your truth!"
~ **Sharifah Hardie**, AskSharifah.com

"This chapter is a great template for artists or any creator who is focused on what they want to do. Staying driven brings purpose and Mr. Green explains that perfectly in this chapter. "
~ **Joe Lavara**, Rolling Stone Specialist

Wow! What an inspiring story. A survivor in so many ways, and to build a successful business after so much adversity is just incredible. Thank you for such an empowering read.
~ **Melissa Desveaux**, Author Consultant, Australia

Book Reviews

I've known and worked with Nor on several projects. She is very well versed with social media marketing and has worked closely with us in implementing strategies that has helped us tremendously.
~ **Dr Frederick Yap**, Founding President, International Business Federation, Singapore

A stirring yet heartwarming read, which encourages, and reminds that there will always be a silver lining if one remains focused on weathering the storm
~ **Hermi Suhirman**, Architect & Landscape Architect, The White Franj-i-panni, New Zealand & Singapore

Nor us very a very inspirational person and always shares what she knows to help others. The wisdom and stories she shares can help anyone regardless of where they are in life. She keeps it simple and to the point. Never feel down and know that you can do anything and learn from those who have gone before to achieve your ultimate goal in life.
~ **Akil Brown**, Internet Marketer Expert, New York

For Nor: your story was so inspiring, it made me humble. Humble in the sense that I viewed what I had achieved and had not with a different set of eyes. It made what I achieved not as great as I thought hence the humility, but it gave me the strength to carry on and pick myself up in spite of these hard times now. I cannot imagine what Nor had gone through with such strength and courage, yet she and her family had been so encouraging and generous with mine. Thank you so much
~ **Dr Yasmin Akrum**, Christchurch Periohygiene Dentist and Periodontist, New Zealand & Singapore

Powerful message for an entrepreneur, never say die in face of hardship because we live on hope. Nor lives with utmost positivity and hope for the future. Congratulations for writing a book to tell us about her experience.
~ **Francis Teo**, Director, Solomon Technologies Pte Ltd, Singapore

Beyond inspiring! A must-read for anyone who has ever faced adversity or doubted their greatness.
~ **Nate Zeleznick**, CEO/Founding Director of Merpati Putih USA and The Vibravision® Foundation, USA

Mike Armstrong inspires everyone he meets. That's what he does! His adventurous spirit enables everyone around him to become more balanced and much stronger in life. In his easygoing manner, Michael, over the years, has effortlessly explained and demonstrated all the various nuances, subtleties, and fine details involving martial arts, business, and life in general. He is a true trailblazer.
~ **Shihan Dana Abbott**, 7th-degree Black Belt, USA

Very raw and inspiring. It provides the reader an opportunity to embark on a new avenue for success. It is a remarkable story of Vandee's own life's struggles turned into victory. It also teaches how to develop a positive mindset, choosing the right people to connect with, and how commitment and consistency in everything that we do in life or in business are what matters most. It's a simple but powerful read for all to find a way to win in life, which the world needs.
~ **Kai Hayes**, Author of *Lion at Heart: Discovering Courage and Greatness Within*, a Leadership, Personal and Spiritual Growth book, and a Global Business Owner and Mentor, USA

Wow! She nailed it! I love how she engaged with the reader's feelings, shared personal experiences, and made it so real! I feel like I can do this! And so inspired to run harder! And be the better version of myself.
~ **Anna Merrill**, Illustrator and Entrepreneur, USA

Spot on! Gratitude, Goals/Vision, Positive Social Circle, and Action is needed to achieve any success. Thanks for sharing!
~ **Lee Vugrenes**, Author of All Things for Your Own Good: An Illegitimate Orphan Korean Boy's Keys to Happiness, USA

Inspiring indeed!
~ **Carolyn Street**, Author, Singapore

This story has given us a great example on how to deal with unexpected situations that happen in our life and turning them into something that comes out even better than expected. 'Your Word Is Law', and delivering the promise is important.
~ **Tanja Malovrh**, Business Strategist, Slovenia

Loving this read. The resilience that Izdihar shows despite setbacks is inspiring to read! How to overcome tragedy and then to turn that into her gift in helping other women thrive.
~ **Juliette Karaman-van Schaardenburg**, Coach, Teacher, Writer on Relationships, Sex and Intimacy, UK

Book Reviews

Incredible read! Dr. Izdihar has an amazing story and a great message of how your word is golden to your growth and to your own truth and identity. My name is Cesar R. Espino, an International Bestselling Author and Mind Coach. As an Entrepreneur, I enjoyed reading her book and the lessons in her book. I highly recommend this book to people. It is a must-read that will empower you on your journey.
~ **Cesar R Espino**, Entrepreneur, USA

"Your Word Is Law"! Never forget that and perfect implementation of the Law of Attraction. Loved the chapter!
~ **Julia Weisenberger**, M.A., Master Storyteller at *The Art of Facebook Storytelling* and #1 International Bestselling Author, Germany

Jess has some true gems in this book. The Mindset foundations laid out are truly inspiring. I admire her journey with such success in the face of such a difficult health situation. It was an honor working with Jess. I am so excited about this book. I highly recommend it!
~ **Colin Fortin**, Corporate Executive, USA

It's practical, actionable, and from Jess Tayel's exceptional experience. If you want to change and transform your mindset truly, read and embrace this book.
~ **Steve Baker**, Transformation Executive, USA

Jess has done an amazing thing sharing her secret sauce in this book. It is eye-opening, inspiring, and powerful actionable advice. Highly recommended and would love a sequel on this.
~ **Jeanne Cole**, Principal Consultant, UK

In her story, Jess Tayel demonstrates a great deal of grit, perseverance, and resilience. To know how much she has been through and yet created such a global business and career before turning 40 is truly inspiring. Thanks, Jess Tayel.
~ **Mark Steward**, Entrepreneur and Executive Coach, Dubai

Such a powerful and empowering book! Jess Tayel has helped me transform my business. My business was struggling, and Jess helped me grow my business and team to a six-figure business, then to seven figures, and laid down the foundations for the team to continue the work. If you want a taste of what it's like to transform your mindset against adversity and difficulty, read this book. Just amazing.
~ **Amanda Clark**, Seven- figure Entrepreneur, Australia and Canada

Nour's story is very inspiring and positive. It illustrates that everyone can overcome challenging circumstances and flourish if they work hard, are sincere and determined, and believe in themselves.
~ **Simon Iskander**, IT Engineer, England

A **must-read** for every person, regardless of creed, race, or color, to reach the zenith of success in whatever field s/he wants to go into. Nour narrates her struggles like a singer captivates the audience with spellbinding performances replete with golden nuggets of wisdom distilled from a thrilling journey.
~ **Dr. Norberto M. Boceta**, DTM, California, USA

Table of Contents

Foreword

Success is a goal that everyone on this planet strives for. Whether sought in a profession, personal life, or health, there are victories to be found in every aspect of life. The struggle for success is a theme that the media, especially social media, has taken advantage of, pumping our brains full of "get rich quick" schemes and endless stories of triumph that leave most of us feeling guilty. What the "gurus" on *YouTube* ads forget to mention when flaunting their mansions is that (1) success won't come overnight, (2) success is entirely relative, (3) it takes courage, commitment, and support to create success.

There is no single key or trick that will shoot you into stardom, but there are proven and time-tested strategies. What I appreciate about this book is the inclusion of 15 different entrepreneurs who have reached success in their own right – and particularly the author! I so appreciate her honest sharing of what she went through herself, and I know the kind of work it takes to compile a book like this…!

No two people have achieved their goals in the exact same way, a truth that *Yes I Can!* highlights perfectly. And what I have read is congruent with my experience.

Each of the 15 entrepreneurs has a dedicated chapter where they've shared their own stories, including the challenges they've faced, the lessons they've learned, and their personal secrets to success. All of them are trailblazers and exemplars for entrepreneurs striving to reach their goals. Mentorship is an important aspect of the struggle for success, and the combined knowledge of these talented entrepreneurs builds a pocket-sized mentor that can be called upon and learned from at any point in the day.

I've been personally inspired by the stories in this book, and my only wish is that you will share the same experience. The entrepreneurs featured took huge steps to gain success and left their comfort zones in the dust. Their courageous actions completely turned their lives around and have paved the way for other entrepreneurs to do the same – just like I did. My challenges were not financial, they were loss, pain, and an environment that was not conducive to any kind of success… yet, I took many of the steps shared here, and the rest, as they say, "is history"…

Susan Fales-Hill said, "If you're too comfortable, it's time to move on. Terrified of what's next? You're on the right track." This quote couldn't describe *Yes I Can!* any better. As entrepreneurs, the odds are all too often stacked against us in the professional world, and unfortunately, the glass ceiling still exists. Actually, there's no country in the world that has total equality for entrepreneurs. It's still a worldwide phenomenon though, in many ways, entrepreneurs do run the world! While success isn't the result of some simple trick, one thing is, in fact, certain: victory in life cannot be obtained within your comfort zone.

I encourage every entrepreneur, regardless of their profession, status, financial condition, or goals, to pick up and read this book in its entirety. The lessons taught and skills shared are transferable to all aspects of life. The entrepreneurs who've shared their stories tell of the obstacles they've toppled, including inequality, lack of support, and mental health.

I wish you tremendous success, and that you may be smart enough to apply what you learn in this book and save yourself years, even decades, of struggles and pain in your journey towards your dreams and goals.

May you continue to be blessed,

Dame Doria (DC) Cordova
CEO / Owner, Excellerated Business Schools® / Money & You®
www.DoriaCordova.com

Introduction

When you look at successful people, have you ever wondered what their secrets are that made them so inspiring? So inspiring, that no matter what happens, they keep moving forward? They seem to just keep expanding their comfort zone and getting more successful. Wouldn't you love to know their secrets so that you can be empowered in your lives too?

The secrets and strategies presented in this book aren't just fancy theories. They have been tested out by real people – just like you and me. More importantly, they produced significant results and have helped them to be successful in their respected fields. You'll start to see that they create their own definition of success which more than the traditional "monetary" beliefs.

Life isn't just about unicorns and roses. We have challenges, dramas, opportunities, and choices. The biggest differences between successful people and ordinary people are the actions that they choose to take despite their circumstances. I believe that we have the vibe and strength within us to be extraordinary in our lives – we just have to learn how to do it.

Success leaves clues. In this book, we will be hashing out the *Mindset Secrets from Inspiring Entrepreneurs Around the World*. The entrepreneurs in this book have walked the path of your story and not only survived but thrived. Some may have been in a much worse condition than you, but they were unstoppable in shifting their life around.

This book brings you the stories of 15 inspiring entrepreneurs from various backgrounds, cultures, and upbringings and will shine a light on what's possible in your life. You are WORTHY of success!

When you implement the ideas and secrets in this book, they will lead you to opportunities and a brighter future.

So, have faith and believe with all your heart that…

"***Yes I Can*** Do This!"

…and your success will follow.

Love,

Izdihar Jamil

Yes I Can!

Dr. Izdihar Jamil

"I manifest my dream life because my word is law!"
~ Dr. Izdihar Jamil

Your Word Is Law

Dr. Izdihar Jamil, Ph.D.
Business Coach, USA

"I manifest my dream life because my word is law!"
~ Dr. Izdihar Jamil

The Unthinkable

"You need to bring your baby upstairs to the 4th flour. We need to prep him for an emergency operation!" the pediatrician told me. My heart stopped. I couldn't breathe. Everything that could go wrong started to flash in front of my eyes. *This can't be happening! It can't be happening!* My son was just 12 months old then. It was just a bad dream.

And yet, I still didn't wake up from it. I was in the ER. It was my reality. I could smell the antiseptic. I saw doctors and nurses in blue and green scrubs running around. I could hear machines going *"beep beep beep"*. I saw people in the waiting room looking gloomy and defeated.

I had brought my son here because he suddenly had developed a huge lump on the back of his neck. He couldn't sleep and was in constant pain. But never in my life had I thought, when I walked into the ER that morning, that my son was about to have an emergency operation just at 12 months old.

I called my husband. I told him to come to the hospital immediately. I felt like a failure for letting this happen to my son. I felt like the worst mom and started blaming myself for all the things I should have done even though I didn't know if there was anything different I could have done. I asked the doctor, *"Can we just not do the operation? Isn't there something else we can try?"*.

"No, there was no other way," the pediatrician said.

My son had developed an infection on his neck that had started to swell like a golf ball and filled with puss. If we didn't remove it, it would spread throughout his body and cause serious health issues. The doctor wanted to remove that puss-filled cyst immediately so his body can heal. *"What if he didn't survive? Oh, God, I can't handle this!"*, I thought. I felt myself crumbling, but the people around me didn't seem to care about my son and me. To them, this was just another "case" to be dealt with.

The Unwanted Calls

As I was settling my son in his cot in the pediatrician wing, I quickly call my Ph.D. supervisor. *"Sri, it's Izzy. I can't go to Finland next week. My son was just admitted to the hospital and needs to undergo an emergency operation!"*, I told him.

*"Oh ****! Don't worry about the trip. Just take care of your son!"* Sri said.

I was supposed to fly off to Finland the next week to collect data and run experiments for my Ph.D. research. I was a Ph.D. candidate at one of the top universities in England. I was researching how children communicate around a digital tabletop in multiple countries, including Finland. Now, there was no way that I could go. Another part of my life shattered. *"If I don't get the data from Finland,* I thought, *how am I going to finish my Ph.D.?"* I could see my career coming down around me as I put my life on hold to be there for my baby.

Next, I called my coach. *"Jenny, I can't come to the seminar this weekend. My son is in the hospital and about to have an emergency operation!"*, I told her. I was supposed to go to London this weekend to attend a mandatory seminar for my leadership training. If I missed it, my leadership training would not be counted because I missed an important milestone. All my hard work for the last six months would be gone. But I knew I had to shut down that part of my life and focus on my son.

I could just have disappeared and brushed things under the carpet. My supervisor and my coach would understand because I was going through a traumatic experience. But something within me said, *"Let me just let them know, and then I can forget about it and focus on my son!"*.

And that's exactly what I did.

The Operation

I remembered carrying my son to the operation theater. I had to lay him down on the operation table. The anesthesiologist said, *"We're going to give him anesthetic, and he's going to go to sleep."* He injected the anesthetic into his IV and started to count backward, *"10, 9, 8, 7, 6, 5…."*. Then, I saw my son, who had been wriggling around in pain, suddenly go lifeless. I knew he was in a deep sleep, yet I felt my heart was being ripped out of my chest.

"What if he never wakes up?", a voice inside my head said.

"Please take good care of him!", I told the doctor as I saw my son being wheeled into the operating theater.

"We will!", the doctor assured me. The odd part of it was that I believed him.

My husband took me out shopping at a crystal shop outside of the hospital to distract me. But of course, I keep worrying about my son. When we were paying for our things, the lady at the counter started to chat with us. We told her that our son was having an operation. She said, *"Ahhh…. So you're just trying to forget things a little bit?".* I thought, *"Trying to, yes, without much success. How can a mom forget that her son is in the operating theater fighting for his life?",* I prayed that God would keep my son safe.

Not long after, we got a call from the hospital. The operation was a success! I was so relieved that my body was shaking. I thank God for His mercy. I went to the operation room and saw my son sitting in front of the computer, watching a video with the nurse. It was as if nothing had happened. He saw me, and he smiled. I could breathe again. He stayed at the hospital for a couple more days for observation before he was discharged.

Finland

Now that my son was safe and healthy, I had to face the s*** that I swept under the carpet while I put my life on hold. Sometimes things always seemed a lot worst after the trauma is over. I got really scared, and I didn't want to deal with it. But if I didn't, I might have had to kiss my Ph.D. goodbye. All that hard work would seem worthless, then.

I went to see my Ph.D. supervisor. *"Sri, my son is safe now. I need to go to Finland to do the research. Can you help me?",* I asked my supervisor.

"Yeah, just go. I'll pay for your tickets!", Sri said. I froze for a moment. All the "drama" in my head turned out to be unreal. I wanted to laugh and cry at the same time.

My supervisor had high expectations, but he was also fair and supportive. He knew I had gone through a big thing with my family, but he also saw my commitment. At that moment, I felt so strong and empowered because I had an amazing supervisor who was supporting me no matter what. He didn't make me feel bad and helped me to make things happen.

I was going to Finland, and I was going to get that data and finish my research. My supervisor bought my ticket to Finland, and I paid for the tickets for my husband and son myself. There was no way I was leaving them behind. The pediatrician had given us the green light that my son could fly, and that was all that I needed.

In Finland, I met with Calkin, my research partner, and together we ran the experiment successfully, She was also my good friend, and she had a son the same age as mine. In a way, that horrible thing that happened led us to something good. When I saw my son smiling and playing with Calkin's son, and my heart was happy. Plus, I got the research data that I needed. *Yay!*

Years after that, my research was accepted at one of the top publication in the world, and I was invited to present my work at one of their most prestigious conferences. You can see my presentation here:

https://www.youtube.com/watch?v=y7jCr6RNXNk

New York

The other part that was left hanging was my leadership training. I was so worried, all I could think about was, *"What was I going to do about that? All my hard work is just about to go up in smoke!"*. One day, I had the dreaded "call" with my head coach Austin.

He told me that they were worried about me and was glad that my son was safe. He laid out for me the choices that I had. Attending the seminar was mandatory for me to successfully complete the leadership training. I missed the London seminar, and the last one for the year was in New York. If I didn't go, then that would be the end of my training.

"New York!!!! You can't expect me to go to New York! My son just had an operation, and I can't leave him. Plus, I don't have the money to pay for the trip. I'm just a student with no income!", I told Austin. I started to put all of my trump cards out there. I wanted them to grant me an exception due to my unexpected circumstances and let me pass. After all I'd been through, I deserved a break.

"Izzy, you can choose to do whatever you want. What you do doesn't make it right or wrong. But, if you value your word like it is gold, like it's the most precious thing in the world, if your word is law, what would it look like? What would you do?", Austin asked me. I was stunned. I felt like I was hit by

a huge wave. I remembered just sitting down and down, and I froze.

Many things flashed in front of me. I sat down and thought a lot about what Austin had just told me. *I signed the agreement saying that I would attend the mandatory training no matter what. Now, who do I choose to be? Someone who gets defeated by circumstances, or someone who would treat her word like gold because it's the most precious thing in the world - because **she** is the most precious thing in the world? I realized it isn't about my coach or New York. It was about **me**. Am I the one that is strong, powerful, and unstoppable, or someone who just gives up?*

I went home and told my husband. He said, *"Go, and I'll take care of our son."*

"Are you sure?", I asked with uncertainty.

"Yes," he said.

All the doubts and fear came to my mind. *Can he really handle my son? Would he know what to do? What if something happened and I'm not there?* I had to let those thoughts go because otherwise, I would spiral down.

Somehow I managed to figure things out with my finances. I booked my flight and hotel in New York and successfully completed my training. *It's amazing once you commit to your word! You start to see solutions to make it happen.*

The beautiful thing was that I started to see my husband as the amazing husband that he truly is. All this while I was pacifying him, and when I let go, I saw that he was able to step in and look after our son probably better than me. They had a great time. I saw the pictures of my son smiling, and I knew that I made the right choices. From then on, I had to freedom to leave my kids with my husband, knowing that they would be taken care of and that they will have a good time.

Little did I know that those life-changing events were to become the fundamental principles I needed to start my online business a few years later. So, my friends, let me share with you how, by honoring my word, I was able to build a successful business in a short period of time. When people talk about manifesting their dreams, I say that I manifested my dream life because *"My word is law!"*. It is done. It's one heck of a story and you're going to love it!

Entrepreneurship

In 2018, I started my coaching and consultancy business after moving to America. I went through horrible social abuse and then started my business as a way of healing from it. I shared about it in my *TED-Ed* presentation, "Turning Fear Into Success." You can check it out here:

https://ed.ted.com/on/3CGIJgOg.

I remember on 13 May of the same year, I went on my first **live** video and challenged myself to commit to doing it for 30 days. It was one of the scariest things that I have ever done. Putting myself out there for the world to judge me is not an easy thing to do, especially since I rarely posted on *Facebook*.

The emotion, the fear, and the challenge were huge, and I wanted to bail out. But I knew that this was what I needed to do to build my audience and accelerate my credibility. Because I said this was something that I'm going to do, I stuck to it. I honored my word because it's priceless. As a result, I rapidly grew my online presence and soon was blessed with amazing clients because of my consistency and persistency. You can read more about my journey in my #1 International Best-selling Book *Yes I Can!* here:

https://www.amazon.com/dp/B08DBHD4HX

…and hopefully, you'll be inspired about conquering your fear.

When I scheduled calls with my clients or prospective clients, I showed up no matter what.

When I book interviews or joint-venture training with other entrepreneurs, I showed up. Is it always like unicorns and roses in my life? Of course not. One thing I learned was that I am a powerful creator in my life.

Does this mean that things are always perfect? Absolutely not. There are times when I messed up, or unexpected things came to my life. But I communicated that the minute I knew that it wasn't working – the same as when my son was at the hospital. I called my supervisor and coach as soon as I could and communicated with them. I applied the same principles here. I then recommit and scheduled another time for me to fulfill my commitment to them. This showed them that I was serious about my work and earned their respect.

During the last few years, I've seen many coaches, clients, and entrepreneurs who scheduled a call with me but didn't show up. Or, they said they were going to do something, but they didn't. The impact of this is that they lose my trust and my feelings of credibility for them. It shows me that they are not taking their life seriously and are just messing around and wasting my time. I get that life happens, but it is not an excuse not to communicate and leave people hanging. Now my business rules are that if they didn't show up, they only get one more opportunity with me. *Why? Because I am priceless. That's how valuable and priceless I am to myself.*

The key here isn't about being perfect and fulfilling 100% of your commitments because there is no such thing. The secret here is to restore your word the fastest way possible and get back in the game every time you fall down. The faster you restore your integrity, the more powerful you become in your life. Because you're telling God not only that you are important, but you also deserve all the success in your life. That is how your word is law. That is how you manifest your dream life because you've shown that you're worthy of it.

The Wisdom

My son's hospitalization significantly changed my life. It was one of my biggest lessons that God wanted me to learn after a life-changing event. Before, I saw myself as weak, and that I just react to things. I didn't have the power to make things happen.

Yet God showed me that even through hardships, I can still rise and be strong, that I had the power to create things in my life. Honoring my word like it's the most precious thing would help me to become someone unstoppable. At that moment, I experienced freedom in my relationship with money, my self-expression, and in my relationship with my husband.

After years of reflection, here are my wisdoms, and I pray that they will shine a light on what's possible in your life:

Wisdom #1: Your Word Is Law

When you say that you're going to do something, commit to doing it 100% no matter what happens. Your word is one of the most priceless things in the world. Incomplete commitments leave you hanging and takes away your strength and power. When you complete things, that gives power, and you feel unstoppable. That's how you manifest your dream life.

Wisdom #2: Restore Your Word as Fast as You Can

When things get messy or unexpected things happen, don't make a big deal out of it. The game is to restore your commitment the fastest way possible. First, you communicate the breakdown to the people involved, so you don't leave them hanging. Second, you recommit back to a time and actions that work best, and you can stick with. Correction without invalidation.

Wisdom #3: You Are a Powerful Creator

You can either be the "victim" or the "winner." You can either "react" or "create" in your life. The truth here is that you have the power to **choose**. Which one do you choose? When you choose to be the creator in your life, you automatically set your mindset towards solutions. "What do I need to do? What actions do I need to take? Who do I need to ask for help? Maybe if I do that, I can get this." What you focus on expands, and it starts with "**Who** do you **choose** to **be**?

Wisdom #4: People in Your Life

The people in your life can make or break your success. I pray to God every day that I am blessed with amazing people that can help me to be successful. I am blessed that my husband supports me in what I do. My supervisor supported me and helped make things possible for my research. My coaches empowered me to be the best versions of myself and keep accountable rather than getting sucked into my drama.

When you have amazing people in your life, always send your gratitude. If you don't, always keep your prayers and have a reflection on whether they are meant to be in your life or not.

Wisdom #5: Have Faith

With every hardship and difficulty, there will be ease. I have faith in God's wisdom in that there are always blessings and lessons in my life. I trusted that goodness, ease, and success will come my way when I am steadfast and commit to my path. I know it can seem crazy to say that, especially when you feel like the world is crushing down on you, but **trust** that miracles will come your way because you are meant for an elevated life.

The Reward

Now my business is stronger than ever. What I made last year I have already smashed through that figure within six months, and I'm still going strong. I'm really thankful for that. I am really blessed to have amazing clients around the world. I love helping women to be bestselling authors within 90 days and help them get into the media, speaking gigs, *TED*, TV, and magazines. I love helping them make their dreams come true and see them having strong credibility and presence within their audience.

If you're interested in learning how to book speaking gigs, media, and *TED* and become the one of the top 10% authorities in your field, join my **free** 3-day course, "The Fast Authority Accelerator" here:

https://www.izdiharjamil.com/fast-authority

I traveled to Bali to attend the Female Entrepreneur Millionaire Retreat and learned from the best in the industry. I hired a red Ferrari F488 for my husband for his birthday. It was his dream car, and I made his dream come true. My kids wanted to eat sushi, and I created the opportunity so that we could go to Japan and have the best sushi. In the summer, we spend our time in Malaysia with my family while I still run my business. I set up my children's education fund and put a structure in place for our retirement.

I have been featured in global media such as *TED-Ed*, *Thrive Global*, *NBC*, Business Innovators, and some of the most high-profile podcasts. I was invited to give a talk at Surrey University in London about my journey from a computer scientist to a successful entrepreneur. I was a guest speaker at the top universities in Malaysia, teaching students how to make money from social media. I am consistently being booked to speak at various international events sharing my expertise and story with thousands of people.

Things didn't just happen for me. It was like *Taaa-daaaa…. Here I am!* I created my vision. I took actions. I honored my word. That's how I created my dream life because I understood the secret that "My word is law!"

My vision for the future is to create a Mastermind and Retreat. I wanted to teach other women how they can create their own publishing and media business and make a lot of money without sacrificing their family life. I'm creating a female entrepreneur retreat at one of the most beautiful islands in the world where women can learn the best business strategies while recharging themselves, and, of course, escape to a little shopping trip to the local market.

I have faith that this vision will come true, and I'm really excited about the things to come. I hope that I have done my best to inspire you and give you hope in your life. I know what you're going through, and I also know that you are meant for an **<u>extraordinary</u>** life!

I'd love to hear your story, so let's connect on *Instagram* (*@izdiharjamil*).

Power Summary

Let's recap the key secrets from this chapter, and I pray that my story will shine a light on what's possible in your life.

1. Fill in the blanks. My word is _____________________

2. Fill in the blanks. I am a powerful _____________________

3. What was one wisdom that I learned from this life-changing experience?

Success Actions

Here are the key actions that you can take to create the life that you desire:

1. What is the one thing you felt was left hanging in your life?

2. List one action that you can take to take the first step in completing that. Write down the date that you are going to do it by.

3. Ask one person in your life to keep you accountable in honoring that action. Have courage and conquer that one action. Tell yourself, *Yes I Can!* and go out there and nail it! You are **<u>unstoppable,</u>** and I believe in **<u>you</u>**!

"With every hardship and difficulty there will be ease. Verily with every hardship and difficulty there will be ease."
~ Quran, 94:5-6.

Love and blessings,

About Me

Dr. Izdihar Jamil, Ph.D., is a former computer scientist turned Business Coach who lives in California with her husband and children.

She loves helping women to become one of the top 10% of authorities in their field by helping them become bestselling authors, getting them booked by the media, speaking gigs, and TED-Ed.

It is her greatest pleasure to see women having confidence in themselves and being successful in their business so they can take care of their families.

Her methods are proven, simple, and effective, and designed to produce the fastest results possible for her clients.

She is also a #1 Bestselling International Author with her books:
She Made It Happen
(http://www.lulu.com/content/paperback-book/she-made-it-happen/26046439),
13 Key Strategies To Make Money Fast In Business
(https://www.amazon.com/dp/1697242979),
Yes I Can!
(https://www.amazon.com/dp/B08DBHD4HX).

She was featured on *TED-Ed,* presenting her story about "The Power of Rejection: Turning NOs into Success."
(https://ed.ted.com/on/ggB51n3V).

In her spare time, she loves reading and baking for her family.

Contacts

Website: www.izdiharjamil.com

Email: izdihar@asaleaday.com

Social Media: Search for "Izdihar Jamil" (*Facebook* and *LinkedIn*), and @*izdiharjamil* (*Instagram*)

Free Gift: 3-day course "The Fast Authority Accelerator":

https://www.izdiharjamil.com/fast-authority

10 Lessons of High Performers

Christian Rey Perez
Masters of Life Podcast, Las Vegas, NV

"How can I leave my mark on the world, I thought, unless I get out there first and see it.."
~ Phil Knight, Nike Founder

"I'm not good at names."

I've said this too many times to too many people. Anyone else?

I used to think that there is no way I could remember the name of every person I met, but I hate to break it to you, the truth is… **Wait!**

Before we get into that, I'd like you to know my story.

*   *   *

I came from a middle-class family with insane-level dreams of being rich. In high school, I knew I wanted to be in business or corporate America. I knew what it took to get there. I loved public speaking, I loved sales, and I loved people. I worked hard in high school, got into college, and took business courses. During college, I got an internship at Enterprise Rent-A-Car, which has a well-respected sales and management program.

Yes, I was just as shocked as you are.

During my time there, I learned that dental, pharmaceutical, and medical device companies **loved** to hire sales reps with Enterprise Rent-A-Car on their resume. I thought, *This is my chance*! *This is how I get rich. This* *is how I make a lucrative career and how I make my parents proud.*

I quickly finished college in three years, which required a lot of summer classes leaving not a lot of social time. I immediately started applying to any company I could find.

I found a dental sales opportunity in Las Vegas, made it to the final interview, and got a call from the regional manager an hour later and then… I didn't get it.

I told the manager, "Look, I'm fresh out of college. I am capable of succeeding in this role. If you have any openings anywhere in the country, I'll take it."

He paused, and then he said, "If you're willing to move to California, I have a position for you there."

I said, "Done!" and the rest is history.

Fast forward two years later…

I needed to be closer to my family for personal reasons, and I landed a job as a medical device rep in Las Vegas. Little did I know, this job was going to push me into my entrepreneurial journey…

*   *   *

I was at the top of my game. I finished college in three years, and I got a $70,000-a-year job right out of college. Two years later, I almost doubled my pay and was living close to home. Then it hit me. My life from high school until then was running 100 miles per hour, chasing the dollar. I was losing my time and my health for the dollar, which was then the driving factor in what I thought would make me happy.

How silly.

The biggest realization came to me as I was driving home from work, exhausted from working for 50 to 60 hours a week for months. I reflected on if I could see myself doing this until I retired. How do I know that I wasn't thinking about my life in my 20s all wrong? What evidence did I have that I was doing the right thing, in the right way, at the right time? My bank account would say yes. My eating, health, happiness, and relationships would say otherwise. If I used my 20s to grow and experiment with what the world has to offer, would I not be better equipped for the next 10, 20, or 30 years of my life? How can I know what truly makes me happy if I don't continue to do things that I am unsure of? If I stay the path of "success" beating myself to the ground, will I truly understand success? At that moment, I knew **I would trade a 6-figure job to find out.**

Before making the jump, you should ask yourself, *Am I prepared for the consequences? What would people think? Would anyone in their right mind do what I'm about to do?*

The answer is simple. **It doesn't matter!**

I had to focus on what I would do once I jump. *How would I gain the insight that I needed to find the meaning of success? How do I meet the people who not only prosper financially but spiritually, emotionally, and physically?* I didn't have the time or money to travel all over the world. I needed a "golden ticket," so to speak.

This is why I started my podcast, *Masters of Life*. I knew I had to meet amazing people from all types of industries to get a new point of view on the world. I needed to learn and grow from different cultures, challenges, and experiences.

Starting a business podcast to interview the most daring, strong-willed, ambitious people has opened my eyes to the possibilities of life and business. Imagine having lunch with a successful person every week. Imagine what you can learn. Imagine the knowledge and opportunities I gained outside of the interview. To gain nothing from another person but their stories and experience saved me **decades** of learning.

*   *   *

Now, about the names. We, as human beings, do not make the conscious choice to remember names. When we meet new people, we focus on what the conversation is going to be and how we are going to respond. We think about ourselves versus taking a genuine interest in them. We **choose** not to be good at names.

Let me give you an example. Have you ever found someone so attractive, and after a conversation with them, you remember everything they said **including** their name? (Don't lie to me.) That's because all you can think about is them. You'll remember what they wore, what they do, even what they smell like!

We often say, "I'm not good at names," to justify to ourselves why we don't remember the people we meet. The truth is you never made the choice from the beginning. If you take anything from a conversation, make it the person's name. You can ask for clarification on anything else, but asking someone, "What's your name again?" is just embarrassing.

When I was in medical sales, after every cold call, my manager would ask me, "What was the front-desk person's name? What was the assistant's name? What was the doctor's name?" He knew how important it was to know everyone's name, even the "little" people. He understood that we can cold call an account three or four times, but we will not gain any traction or build any meaningful connection if we do not know the names of who we were talking to. How can we expect to sell, to connect, to make someone feel important, without first knowing something as simple as their name?

Dale Carnegie says it best,

"Remember that a person's name is to that person the sweetest and most important sound in any language."

Dale Carnegie is famous for writing the book *How to Win Friends and Influence People*, which I highly recommend you read if you haven't already. It is a staple in the business and entrepreneur world.

Why do I bring this up? Why is this so important to me? This is the first major lesson I learned in my career, and it is the foundation of any worthwhile relationship.

*   *   *

I have interviewed *Shark Tank* entrepreneurs, cybersecurity/finance CEOs, life coaches, social activists, *Inc. Magazine* entrepreneurs, distinguished Ted speakers, toastmasters, politicians, million-dollar podcasters, luxury real estate moguls, international best-selling authors, social media icons, Las Vegas performers, and Silicon Valley superstars.

I want to share with you the 10 mindset lessons that I found to be the most impactful from my interviews. I tried to avoid the cliché, I tried to avoid the cheesy, and I tried to avoid anything that you could see on a motivational social media post.

No appetizer, no salad, all entrée.

1.   Differentiate Between Real and Imagined Threats

The most successful understand what they need to worry about and what they'll do when it happens. They create a fine line between what they can control and what they can't.

The whole purpose is to live in the **present**. Focus on what actions you can take. We have limited capacity in what we can worry about, so it's best to direct that energy away from the **perceived** future.

Business will throw many variables your way but be mindful and purposeful about what you give your attention to.

"Worry never robs tomorrow of its sorrow, it only saps today of its joy."
~ Leo F. Buscaglia, Author and Motivation Speaker

2. Command Your Circle

This lesson is about creating opportunities for yourself. Too many of us entrepreneurs will go out and try to find mentors or professionals that we want to learn from. This is amazing, but don't forget, **you** are amazing too!

Too many of us want to be "at the table," but the best way to sit with who you want is to invite others! It is possible to have access to whoever you want, but you have to **believe** that your table is worth sitting at.

This is also the basic concept for masterminds, which I strongly suggest everyone joins. A mastermind is a group of people that meet regularly to talk about ideas, problems, and solutions. It is a coalition of minds which is much more powerful than any one individual.

"You're the average of the five people you spend the most time with."
~ Jim Rohn, Motivational Speaker

3. Conflict is Essential

There's a level of humility in listening and learning, especially from people you compete with or disagree with.

Disagree – Being open-minded is one of the hardest things to do because humans have too much **pride**. We love to prove our point and make sure people know our point of view. But the question you constantly have to ask is, *How do I know that I am right?* This isn't self-doubt, but rather a quest for validation. Open your mind to weigh the facts and then make a decision.

Compete – Simon Sinek, in his new book, *The Infinite Game*, talks about "worthy rivals." Instead of focusing on your competition as someone to beat, think about them as who you can learn from, who you can grow from, and who you can ultimately outlast. Learn their strategies and make them your own. Pivot and adapt.

"Any fool can know. The point is to understand."
~ Albert Einstein, Physicist

4. Business is a Potluck

This lesson is about understanding that everyone must carry their own weight. As business owners, we continually feel responsible for our employees. We constantly care more about the business than those around us. (Which makes sense, right?) But creating a team that believes in you and wants to see you succeed is the key to a strong foundation.

Don't feel that you have to bring the "food" every time. You are doing a disservice to the growth of your team if you constantly "feed" them. Teach your team to be resourceful. Teach your team to hunt. Teach your team to survive.

"Train people well enough so they can leave, treat them well enough so they don't want to."
~ Richard Branson, Virgin Founder

5. Resourcefulness is the Main Ingredient

Hard work never goes out of style. If you think someone is more talented, has an advantage over you, has more money than you, what is your reaction?

The only correct answer is… you are **motivated**.

Resourcefulness is the strongest skill anyone can have,

especially entrepreneurs. I've never met anyone who was resourceful and also envious of others.

Envy is a form of acceptance, and many "wantrepreneurs" have this thought of "if only." That mindset is the death of progress. I am guilty of this. I thought that to start a podcast, I would need to know people and have great connections. (It made me start my podcast two months after the idea.) But we all start somewhere and build. It's easy to forget the build. It's easy to quit.

Remember, those that succeed are the ones that outlast their competition. Business is a cycle, and it is an "infinite game," as Simon Sinek puts it.

Just keep working and believing.

"Work like there is someone working 24 hours a day to take it away from you."
~ Mark Cuban, Entrepreneur

6.   Patience is a Form of Action

Learn to love the journey and hard work. Learn to love the process of failure and fighting through the challenges. Being patient is an understanding that it will all pay off.

Work on your craft every day, slowly getting better than the day before. Remember, owners were once founders, teachers were once students, and pros were once amateurs.

"The day you plant the seed is not the day you eat the fruit."
~ Fabienne Fredrickson, Founder of BoldHeart

7.   Be Prepared to Accept Opportunity

What is the purpose of opportunity if you don't **grab** it! As entrepreneurs, there is so much freedom that it is important that you look into all the possibilities that will help you grow your business. Not in a million years did I think I would be writing in a book, but I quickly learned the credibility someone can gain by having a book.

The biggest key to this lesson is time management and organization. You have to set up your buckets to receive the rain. Otherwise, you won't have any time to do anything with it. When you are organized and precise with your business, and you run it versus it running you, you open yourself up to capitalizing on opportunities.

"You get to decide where your time goes. You can either spend it moving forward, or you can spend it putting out fires. You decide. And if you don't decide, others will decide for you."
~ Tony Morgan, Author

8. Believe in Something Bigger than Yourself

It might sound tacky at first but knowing your "why" and your purpose is the mindset I found to be the most common among my guests. You have to believe in something. There is no fulfillment in constantly achieving personal goals. As beginning entrepreneurs, freedom and hard work are enough to give us purpose.

However, as you reach certain milestones in your business, money is not a sustainable motivator. You must believe that what you're doing is bigger than who you are. It could be your employees, it could be your family, and it could even be social change. What will get you out of bed is knowing that someone is depending on you. Impacting others will be the key to finding satisfaction in what you do.

"Happiness is really just about four things: perceived control, perceived progress, connectedness (number and depth of your relationships), and vision/meaning (being part of something bigger than yourself)."
~ Tony Hsieh, Founder of *Zappos.com*

9. Don't Settle for a Life Less than what You Are Capable of Living

Make your goals supernatural. Make it exciting. Make it scary. Make it **big, hairy, and audacious!** …as Jim Collins puts it.

If you know in your gut that you don't see yourself doing what you're doing now, take that leap. Take that chance. Strive for more. Realizing that so much is possible when you decide that you are capable of it. That's what entrepreneurship is all about!

"Have the courage to follow your heart and intuition. They somehow already know what you truly want to become. Everything else is secondary."

~ Steve Jobs, Apple Co-founder

10. Be Successful as a Human Being

The last lesson is what I strive for every day.

Humility, integrity, kindness, and generosity is something we should all work towards and look for in others. Cutting corners and treating people as if they're below you will not get you the people that you need. It might help you make money fast, but like I said earlier, money won't give you lifelong fulfillment.

Throw away your pride. Throw away the thought of being more successful than your neighbor. Throw away the thought of money will define your success. Focus on the right things, and you will attract the right things.

The theory of the compounded effect holds true to be a better human being. Make the hard choices every day to be kind and patient with those around you. Make the hard choice of choosing the right thing to do, even if it'll take your success a little longer. Make the hard choice to take the road less traveled. Do yourself a favor and clear your mind of the thoughts of envy, greed, and pride.

Make friends and connections that last a lifetime because "success" is defined by how you impact those around you. It is defined by how those closest to you will remember you after you're gone from this world.

"Good ethics is good business."
~ Anonymous

This is your time to make a change. This is your time to change the way you think. This is your time to make the conscious decision to be better. It doesn't happen overnight, but progress is progress. Every day you get better, every day you **decide** to be a better human being. Work towards leaving a job that makes you unhappy. Spend more time thinking about what will give you fulfillment, then **execute**.

I will continue to learn and grow from my amazing guests, and I have a long journey ahead of me. I don't know exactly what it will bring, but it **sure** is exciting to think about.

Finally, to whoever is reading this, I wish you the strength, the wisdom, and the discipline to achieve all your goals, but most importantly, I wish you the joy that the process brings.

"Most people overestimate what they can do in one year and underestimate what they can do in ten."
~ Bill Gates, Microsoft Founder

Best of luck,

Christian Rey Perez

About the Author

Christian Perez is the founder of publicity-based, networking platform, MasterCrowd and host of the Masters of Life Podcast. He was a medical device rep before he quit to pursue entrepreneurship.

He lives in Las Vegas, Nevada, with his girlfriend of nine years and mini Goldendoodle, and would love to connect if you are ever in "Sin City." He loves to play chess and basketball in his free time.

He is passionate about organizations like Operation Underground Railroad (focuses on stopping child trafficking) and the National Lymphedema Network (focuses on the treatment and awareness of lymphedema).

Contacts

Email: Christianp@mastercrowd.io
Christianp@mastersoflifepodcast.com

Website: Mastercrowd.io
  Mastersoflifepodcast.com

Instagram: @Christianrey_perez
@MasterCrowd

Facebook: https://www.facebook.com/christian.perez.3766952

LinkedIn: https://www.linkedin.com/in/christian-rey-perez-570aa9a5/

Linktree: linktr.ee/mastersoflifepodcast

Flirting with Forever

Ellie Erickson
Dating and Relationship Coach, USA

"Know yourself, know your worth."
~ Aubrey Drake Graham

It's Not You, It's Me

The Starbucks napkin was a rough substitute for a proper tissue, but beggars can't be choosers when you weren't expecting to have a crying fit in your car. You know the kind, the type of episode where your car offers the closest thing to privacy you can get when you need to have a breakdown. I was in college, and wondering how I kept ending up in relationships, or "situation-ships," with people who weren't healthy partners. They weren't terrible by any means, but why did I keep finding myself in the same situation – empty and confused?

I had just gone through a breakup with someone who I adored. It was "mutual" enough, but breakups are hard, even when you know somewhere deep down, it's probably for the best.

I started thinking about my life. *Was this a pattern in more ways than just romantically? Did I allow relationships and situations into my life that didn't serve me outside of only matters of the heart and not professionally, platonically, and practically everywhere else?*

I quickly realized that I was allowing behavior from boyfriends that wasn't acceptable. But of course, I could make an excuse for anything! *Not responding in a reasonable amount of time? Well, they're a workaholic! How admirable! Don't want to commit? We're young! And we all need to focus on ourselves, right?*

But then, when I sat down to reflect, I realized this pattern of making excuses for people who couldn't bother making them for themselves stemmed from growing up in a home where alcoholism and addiction took priority over everything else – growing up in a house where chaos was the norm, excuses became a survival method. They didn't **mean** to kick the door down; it was the alcohol. They didn't **really mean** what they said; they were drunk. They **wanted** to come to the band recital, but they had been given a DUI. Anyone who has loved an addict in any way knows that life with them is a roller coaster. The highs are the best moments of your life, but the lows leave you broken and wondering where *you* went wrong.

Growing up, I really struggled with always coming in second to a bottle. How could a parent choose a substance over someone who looked up to them for everything? So, of course, excuses and the belief that love looked like this whirlwind of massive mistakes, and then beautiful apologies, were what I came to believe. I knew love to be gorgeous disorder. So, I allowed behavior from friends, family, and eventually boyfriends that modeled what I grew up with. Drama was my baseline, and when things were healthy and stable – well… that just felt so boring! So, I kept attracting situations into my life that would have been a better fit for the *Lifetime Movie Network*.

A New Playlist

I was over it. You get to a point where enough is enough, and the drama is less exciting and more of a catalyst for leading a stable life where you just **don't have to deal with it anymore**. I scrolled through my *Spotify* music and stumbled on a playlist labeled "Workout." I was still sitting in my car in some random parking lot, far from any squat racks and ellipticals. Still, I knew the vibe was exactly what I needed to pump myself up and get me feeling less helpless. This was the type of playlist sprinkled with some Beyonce, E-40, and Taylor Swift circa "Red." Out of the speakers, I heard Drake rapping about going from zero to 100 "real quick", and then he spoke the magic words…

"Know yourself, know your worth."

I paused. The Starbucks napkin dropped onto the seat next to me, and I thought to myself, *What does it mean to know yourself and know your worth?* I popped open the glove compartment and all of the registrations and car insurance cards from the past five years spilled onto the floor. I should really organize this. God forbid I ever get pulled over. Sifting through them – I know it's in here somewhere – got it! I grab the miniature notebook tucked away, a gift from a career fair with some company's logo on the front I don't recognize. I find a pen on the floor of the back seat and start writing.

First, know yourself. Think, think, think… *What do I know about myself?*

I'm resilient. I'm really good at observing people. I can engage a room full of people when I'm on a stage. Kids love me. I'm a fantastic listener. I love helping others.

The list kept flowing. I sat for thirty minutes and wrote out all the things I knew about myself that I loved. There were some pauses. Sometimes I would think that I ran out of things, but I challenged myself to continue, even when I thought that I was ten lines past finished. Once I sat back and looked at the pages full of things I had to be proud of, I started to understand how knowing myself could help me realize my worth. Our worth doesn't come from what we do or what our strengths are. Our worth comes from the simple act of existing. However, when we don't really believe that internally, these lists can help considerably in showing ourselves that we actually are fantastic beings worthy of being treated with respect, love, and compassion.

I continued the list of things I loved about myself on the notes section of my phone. That way, even on-the-go, I could add to it. In line at Target, pumping gas, at work – I realized more and more things I had to be proud of. Why? Because I was making a conscious effort to look for them, and we always find what we're looking for. In the quiet moments where I began to doubt myself, I would pull out the list to remind myself of all my strengths and of all the reasons I was more than capable of overcoming challenging things and changing the narrative I had been brought up in.

You Teach Others How to Treat You

I believe more than anything that you teach people how to treat you. When you start believing in your own strengths and knowing your worth, you start to teach people that you deserve to be treated with respect and love.

I started dating again, and my new findings were transformative. The guys would text me back almost immediately. They would make time for me, and they respected my boundaries. Why? Because I knew myself and knew my worth. I was **teaching** these people that I was someone to be taken seriously and to be treated as a priority. And the ones that didn't treat me that way? The magic of it is that they didn't last very long because I made the conscious decision to remove them from my life, because **I knew they weren't learning the lesson I was teaching them**. I dropped them from the class that is my life. It was that easy.

Attracting My "Happily Ever After"

Eventually, I met my current partner, who is the most loving man I have ever met. He always respects my boundaries and understands the importance of stability and consistency. He surprises me with kind gestures, and possibly most important for me coming from the home situation I did, he shows up – every time. When I need him to, when I don't, he's there. He's at the airport with flowers, at every speaking engagement. He's the first to stand and clap when I take a bow on stage. He shows up on December 25th, but more significantly, he shows up on March 12th, and all of the other random Tuesdays that are less glamorous when we still need someone in our corner.

Sometimes, I think about how tragic it would have been if I had continued my behavior pattern of allowing situations into my life that didn't serve me. If I hadn't spent the time to know myself and realize my worth, I would never have ended up with someone as wonderful as I now have. I would have continued to fall for people who were less than deserving because I had that internal belief that I was less deserving also.

I hope that my story of internal transformation can offer some inspiration for you to enter your own metamorphosis. I would love to share more on how I decided to continue my learning in regards to dating and relationships and ultimately turned it into a profession.

A Little Backstory

I grew up in the Bay Area in California, an area known for its innovativeness, diversity, and high rent prices. It was incredible to grow up somewhere with so many different ideas and perspectives. I spent a lot of time living with my grandparents, which was an incredible gift because grandparents have a different perspective than parents. They have more life experience, and that gives them a swagger that screams, "I've seen this before, and if I know anything, it's that things are going to be okay."

Something I have come to value most from growing up is that mindset. Whenever I start to feel overwhelmed with the little intricacies of life, I try and jump in a mental time machine and imagine myself in a rocking chair, looking back at my own life. I think of the stories that I'll have to tell my own grandchildren. I make decisions that will make my grandkids go, "That's so cool!" when I tell them about the things I have done. I always come to the understanding that these problems that now seem life-ending are going to be little blips on the radar in 60 years.

After going to college at Cal Poly in San Luis Obispo, I decided to move across the country for a job in Florida. Although lovely, the alligators were too much for me... that, and I was ready for another adventure. I decided to move across the country again, and then across an ocean and ended up in

Maui, Hawaii, another push outside of my comfort zone. Those experiences are always challenging, but it's those that end up being incredibly beneficial because, in the most challenging situations, we prove to ourselves what we are really capable of.

I had a bit of an advantage moving to Maui because my partner moved there with me! We had been doing a long-distance relationship for a year while he worked in Portland, Oregon, and I survived the humidity in Orlando, Florida. We were living together for the first time and were thriving in our relationship. My friends, and even strangers, started asking me how I attracted such an amazing person into my life and how we had such an awesome relationship. I started creating informational videos about dating and relationships on *Youtube*, and then I started getting requests for private coaching. That is how I started my current coaching practice!

Coaching on Love and Life

Although I do classify myself as a dating and relationship coach, I focus on the lessons I had to learn the hard way, the ones that have to do with ourselves, rather than someone else. I incorporate all the research I have done throughout college and the years after. I've spent thousands of hours reading books, listening to podcasts, and interviewing the professionals on the science of dating, relationships, and mindset. I get to introduce my amazing clients to attachment theory, energy styles, boundaries, the value in daily practices, the best ways to show up on dates and dating apps, and so much more! It's my absolute dream job because I get to remind people that while entering into a healthy relationship requires inner work, the process of dating and doing that inner work can be **so much fun**.

Having been named by *Yahoo Finance* as one of the Top-ten Life Coaches of 2020, getting approached to be in books like the one you're reading now, and working with other coaches and entrepreneurs around the world – it's clear that it was all worth it! I am overwhelmed with gratitude every time I think about how far I have come, and how I get to have a similar impact on my clients **every single day**.

When I look back, it becomes indisputable that the moment I realized I needed to know myself and my worth in order to change the patterns that continued to repeat themselves in my world was the moment that **actually** changed my life. The key lessons I've learned can be found below, and my wish for you is that you have your own realizations and create the life you've always dreamed of.

Lasting Thoughts

1. Understand that growth is a process. I didn't wake up the day after starting my list and jump out of bed feeling 100% confident with myself and like I was ready to take on the world! The beautiful thing about a lifetime is that we can, and should, grow **<u>every single day</u>**. I'm still growing, and all of the most self-aware and inspiring people I have known share that same mentality.

2. You're going to have hard days, even when you're doing everything right. That's life. Even after I made my list, even when I started dating quality people, even when I was doing all the inner-work, there were still times where I struggled. The most important thing is how you look at those hard days. Did they happen to break you? Or did they happen so you could break the mold of what you used to think you could overcome? Framing it in your head to be the latter will get you much further.

3. Stepping outside of your comfort zone is absolutely terrifying. It is also absolutely necessary. Thinking about moving across the country or an ocean? Do it! To be daring will be one of your greatest strengths. If I had allowed myself to not take risks and stay in the comfort of what I knew, I would not have had nearly as many exciting life experiences. My future grandkids would be remarkably bored if I tried telling them stories of my life while living inside the safe expectations of others.

The "Happily Ever After"

I now have a confidence that allows me to take risks and do scary things because I know that even if things don't work out the way I want them to, I'll be able to handle it. I have an understanding with myself that if someone or a situation isn't beneficial for my mental wellbeing, it gets removed! Having done the internal work, and continuing to do so, allows me to show up for my clients and for everyone in my life in my most authentic way. The only way we should be showing up!

My days now involve coming home to flowers on the table and waking up to notes on the nightstand, reminding me that I am loved. On my worst days, there's my favorite ice cream in the freezer, a quick stop off on my partner's way home from work. On my best days, I have someone to call who will be just as excited about my wins as I am. There's a quiet peace in our home, and there are no excuses for poor behavior. There's consistency and routine, something I wasn't used to. There is never a shortage of laughter, and whether we're walking on the beach or shopping for groceries at Costco, we have the **best** time. He's my favorite person to go on adventures with, and he's the person that I can count on to support me through the toughest times life will bring. It's a relationship I only used to dream of. If only I had known earlier that this type of love was possible!

And it's possible for you too, I promise!

Power Summary:

Let's recap some of the key points in this chapter:

1. You teach others how to _______ ____.

2. What did I have to learn in order to enter a healthy relationship?

3. What happened after I made a list of my strengths?

4. Knowing the tools that were most helpful, I'm going to list them below so you can try them for yourself, and I'm confident if you take these steps, you can experience the same transformation.

Success Actions

1. **Make. The. List!**

    Write out the little things like "I make **the best** brownies," and the big things like "I inspire others to live their best lives." This exercise will start to train your mind to look for the things you're good at, and soon you'll be walking around with all the confidence in the world.

2. **Be Clear on Your Boundaries**

    Creating boundaries for what you will allow from others will help you stick to them when a situation arises that makes you wonder what you should do. This might look like "If someone doesn't change their behavior after I tell them I don't like it, then I will make sure that person is not present in my life."

3. **Start Your Day with Gratitude**

    Just like creating a list of your strengths will train your mind into looking for qualities you have to be proud of, creating a gratitude list will train your mind to look for things you have to be grateful for throughout the day. And like magic, when you start to notice these things throughout the day, more and more of them start to show up!

"To love oneself is the beginning of a life-long romance."
~ Oscar Wilde

Love Always,

Ellie Erickson

About the Author

Ellie Erickson is a dating and relationship coach based out of Hawaii, but working with women all around the world.

Her passion lies in inspiring others to grow daily, live daringly, and connect authentically. She does this primarily through working with women in uncovering their limiting beliefs around love, and getting them to a place where they are excited about dating again and ready to enter the relationship they've always dreamed of!

Contacts

If you are interested in learning more, head over to her website at :

https://ellieerickson.co/

Connect on *Instagram* @EllieErickson:

https://www.instagram.com/ellieerickson/

For further inquiries, feel free to reach out via email to:

Ellie@EllieErickson.co

I am extremely grateful for my family and friends who have supported me as I stepped into this exciting place I have found myself. There have been lots of unknown variables, and your encouragement as I navigate new spaces has been such a gift.

You Are the Driver in Life and Business

Gabriele Grikstaite
Ecommerce Consultant, Copenhagen, Denmark

"When you decide to take charge of your own mind, you'll have actual superpowers."
~ Gabriele Grikstaite

So, now what? I kept repeating the question over and over again in my head while mustering the courage to get out of bed. It was 12.30 p.m. on a Tuesday. I had been lying in bed all day every day for almost two months straight. The truth was no one really knew **how** rough my life really was. In two short and yet painfully long years, I had suffered a whirlwind of losses and setbacks, and now I was stuck in my head with severe health problems and no money in my bank account.

I remembered when I was mentally preparing to quit my corporate career job and decided to confront my worst fear – driving a car in the South of France. Considering my fear of driving, I had thought to myself, *If I can overcome this crazy adventure on my own, I'll be able to overcome **anything** life throws at me as an entrepreneur*. Taking a good cut in my savings, I booked my ten-day, solo trip and rented a ridiculously expensive car. "I'd rather crash in style than playing it safe and boring in a worn-out vehicle," was my motto. And off I went up and down narrow mountain roads with sweaty palms and a racing heart while praying for my life.

After a solid ten days of nerve-wracking adventures, I handed over the car keys to the rental company with a smooth smile on my face. I was still alive! That means I'd done something right, for sure!

I still had the same mix of upsetting anxiety and unwavering determination as I lay in my bed two years later, wondering how to get back on track in my life and business. I **had** quit my corporate job and ventured out on my own. I hadn't known anyone who'd done that before, and to be fair to myself, I had actually made **some** kind of living for myself during the two years I had been in business. That's statistically longer than the average entrepreneur makes it for here in Denmark. I practised this kind of positive self-talk again and again, but the anxiety and immobility still didn't go away.

The fear was crippling me. What if this was it? What if loneliness, anxiety, and complete burnout was the price I'd have to pay to make it as an entrepreneur?

The thing was, I'd actually taken out a new driver's license – a new, real-life license of starting a business – and now I was scared of driving all over again!

Because the road ahead was unknown to me, I was sure that I'd have a terrible crash as soon as I pressed the gas pedal and moved ahead with my business. Because, truthfully, the two previous years had been a **terrible**, nerve-wracking learning experience. But the longer I kicked the tires and was overthinking **everything**, the more of a disservice I was doing to my life and business. Catastrophizing thoughts were trapping me big time! It was time to embark on a new car ride to the South of France, I decided. This time, in my own life and business.

I still remember the morning of the day that I decided to get out of my head and back on the road. I had been joining weekly coaching sessions online, (the perfect place to start while hiding from real life under your bedsheets), and learned something that blew my mind: All successful entrepreneurs have faced adversity **many** times over, but the ones that truly have success have learned to keep going by navigating the road signs of life and business. Wow! There were actual road signs? Why hadn't I learned to navigate those?!

Suddenly, my plan of action was very clear. I needed to decode those signs immediately in order to drive without crashing, and I knew **exactly** where to start!

This particular morning, I finally got out of bed, put on a very businessy attire, and chucked down a cup of coffee. It was me versus the road, so, let's go! I wasn't even nervous as I rushed to a client site I hadn't visited for a very long time. The project I was working on had fizzled out, and I knew my chances of keeping the client were poor. Without hesitation, I made my way to the CEO's office and bluntly blurted out, "I know you're not entirely happy about my services. What's troubling you?"

I was about to decode the first road sign. How exciting!

As I started to understand the road signs and react accordingly, I started to tweak things for myself and my clients, the business services that I offered, the people I took advice from, and, most importantly, I was no longer trapped in catastrophizing thoughts! The rest is more or less history. When I found out **exactly** what my client wanted, I turned their e-commerce business around in three months and started to really gain confidence in myself and traction in my business.

At the end of my second year in business, I had earned more than I would have at my corporate job. That was such an amazing feeling! Had I trapped myself in my head, I would not have found the secret that was the turning point in my business. I learned that in anything, it is important to keep practising and give it time for the results to unfold.

Don't Overthink the Road Signs

One day when I was working on the three-month e-commerce turnaround project, everything came crashing down. I panicked big time! I thought about every possible worst-case scenario that could unfold. Instantly, I pictured myself curled up in bed, feeling like a complete disaster. Now that I was back on the road taking action and giving it my all, failure was such a huge blow to me! With tears in my eyes, I looked through the course materials from my online coaching sessions. This **had** to be a road sign to be conquered, and then it dawned on me!

Imagine driving on a road and seeing a stop sign appear. Would an experienced driver go into full panic mode and think, *Oh my dear Lord! There's a stop sign! OMG! OMG! OMG! What should I do?*

No way! A confident driver would look at the sign, act accordingly, and then only proceed when it's safe to do so. Maybe they'd even hum along to a song on their playlist while navigating in complete autopilot mode. So, that's what I did. I put on my favourite playlist, and cheerfully continued to fix every issue until the road was clear, and it was safe to drive again.

Sounds much better than being stuck in panic mode, right?

This lesson taught me that road signs will always appear in different places, shapes, and forms, but once you have passed your driver's license test, you will keep calm and know **exactly** what to do when you see a certain type of sign. It will be so deeply rooted in you that you don't even register it consciously. That's what your mindset in business should look like!

I now have the confidence to sing along to my favourite playlist while driving down undiscovered roads, because I know that I don't have to overthink every sign on my way. Navigating cheerfully through uncertain terrain has allowed me to be confident in my skills, grow my business, and make much more money for my clients and me than ever before.

Who would have thought that getting out of my head would make me feel so much better even in the most challenging situations?

The Ordinary World

I am sharing what I've learned, hoping it will bring value to your undertakings in life. I've been told that words of wisdom resonate even better when there is a real, relatable human being behind them. So here is my "why" of ditching my career as a marketing consultant at a global consulting firm and jumping into entrepreneurship.

I was born in Lithuania, a country blessed with exceptional natural beauty and extremely resilient people. Until age three, I lived in a three-bedroom apartment, together with the majority of my family – eight people and a Dobermann crammed together. It was a total mess, and I loved it! Those are some of my fondest childhood memories. When my parents went through a horrible divorce, however, my world was instantly turned upside down.

At age six, I moved to Denmark together with my mom as she had gotten engaged to a Danish businessman. I had to adapt to a completely new life situation, culture, and language. For several years we lived a very privileged and carefree life, but I learned that nothing is constant in life. My stepfather's business came to a halt, and during the majority of my teenage years, my family was barely getting by.

One of the most significant values that I learned growing up in an ever-changing environment was to always work hard at creating my own opportunities. I learned not to take anything for granted, because, even if life was moving along nicely, I knew that it could all come crashing down without warning. So, the best way to prepare for anything in life was to cultivate the ability to bounce back. Education was my weapon of choice. I graduated from high school with such a high GPA that it was featured on national TV. Today, I have a Master's Degree in Branding and Communications

Management from Copenhagen Business School, having supplemented my studies at highly prestigious universities in both Tokyo and New York.

My lifelong preparation was tested to the extreme barely one year into my first full-time career job. I was working in a horrible environment with daily harassment and **hated** my life with passion! But it was nothing compared to the rock bottom I hit when my dearly beloved stepfather was diagnosed with terminal cancer. That's when I realized that spending time with your loved ones is the only thing that truly matters in life.

I quit my corporate job and started building a consulting business that could be managed from home. During my first year in business, I was juggling the emotions that come with the ups and downs (mostly downs) of terminal illness and subsequent loss.

I know that turbulent times require a lot of positivity and support. Through my company, <u>Ecommerce Superpowers</u>, I now help creative individuals turn their passions into profitable, e-commerce businesses under the motto "No more sleepless nights worrying about your e-commerce business."

Key Lessons and Words of Wisdom

Looking back, I now know that in life and business, you have to be able to read the road signs and keep driving. Once I got out of my head, I was able to set my business and life up for success. I was more successful with my clients, made more money, and, most importantly, I was having much more **fun** doing it!

I'm humbled to share the key lessons and mindset hacks I have used to overcome adversity. I sincerely hope that they will help you get in the driver's seat of your own life and business.

Wisdom #1 — Stop Waiting for the "Perfect" Time to do X, Y, and Z

<u>Now</u> is the perfect time to do anything! We live in a beautiful era with plenty of opportunities. Technology has enabled literally anyone with an Internet connection to start turning their passions into profits. Life will never stop happening and give you the perfect, quiet, secure moment to start your own business. Give yourself permission and get going! I started at a **horrible** time in my personal life, but it was actually the business aspect that got me going. Knowing that I was in charge of building my own dream life was extremely empowering! If I could do it during those circumstances, you can

<u>**definitely**</u> do it too. You got this!

Wisdom #2 — Start Humbly, but Dream Big

You don't need a huge office, the right logo, website, or business card to start a business, but dreaming **big** is an absolute must! It will make all obstacles look minor. Trust me; you'll thank me later.

Wisdom #3 — Get Expert Help

Would you feel secure driving a car without prior driving lessons? That's exactly what I felt like when I ventured out on my own. I realized that I had absolutely no clue on how to turn the engine on in my business. I had endless questions like, how to actually attract paying clients, which services to offer, and how to price them. Safe to say, I was clueless.

Looking back, what I have invested in expert help has now given me a return of at least ten times more! I saved myself the frustration, many sleepless nights, and money by hiring experts for the areas that I needed help with, and I am so thankful for that.

Wisdom #4 – Take Action

Action produces results. Actions are the connector between your thoughts and the outer world. Yes, we can all sit back and hope for the best, but action is the key to turning those dreams into reality. No matter how frightening, stupid or "not you" an action is, just do it! Only practice makes perfect. And practice involves a thousand imperfect attempts. So you better embrace the wonderful journey of "f***ing" up on a regular basis. That's the only way towards your destined success.

Wisdom #5 – Looking Back Down the Road

When faced with a challenge, stop and imagine having reached your destination after a beautiful drive. Does your challenge look major or minor when you look back down the road? Often, when we put a long horizon on challenges, decisions become much more clear. How do you want **<u>your</u>** journey to have looked like once you come to the end of the road?

Wisdom #6 — Remember to Fuel Up

A car cannot drive without the right fuel. Remember that you need the right fuel to function too. In the early days, when my business and personal life was in absolute chaos, I thought it was important to hustle through regardless of the signals my body was trying to give me. Ouch! That proved to be the costliest business mistake of all! Remember, when starting up, you are your business. If you're not well fuelled (we're talking body, mind, and soul here!), how do you then expect to drive your business to success?

Wisdom #7 — Keep Believing in Your Ability to Figure it Out

Always have courage and faith in yourself. Even when things seem impossible, know that you have the strength and power within to figure it out. When you focus on solutions, you immediately trigger a sense of curiosity, adventure, and fun. Now, isn't that more exciting than getting yourself all wound up? I surely think it is!

The Reward

Today, I am reaping the rewards of having taken charge and ventured out on the entrepreneurial road. My business is getting stronger, running more smoothly, and it is truly fulfilling to see the rewards my clients get from my services. I get to work with incredibly inspiring and passionate creative people around the world – and, if I want to, I can run my business from my couch!

Now, I get to enjoy my favourite kind of holidays - offseason travelling, when the major influx of tourists have left and leave room for an authentic experience, because I can take time off when I want to. This year, I am going to buy my own apartment in Copenhagen. The downpayment is already secured, and the bank has approved the loan. Yay! Also, as a wonderful perk of working with many female-focused brands, my wardrobe is now booming with more designer wear that I could possibly have dreamt of. (I'm like the designer wear rent-point for my little sister and girlfriends.)

When you become the driver in your own life and business, you'll be invincible! You'll start to see amazing things happen, and more importantly, you become healthier and happier. So, get into that car, start driving, and trust that a beautiful road will unfold.

Power Summary

Let's recap some of the key points in this chapter:

1. Fill in the blank. My mindset is my actual ________

2. What was the key lesson that I learned when I started to decode the road signs?

3.   What was the impact on my business when I chose to get out of my head and back on the road?

Success Actions

Here are the three success actions that I recommend to supercharge your life and business:

1.   Get out of your head, **<u>now!</u>**

2.   Commit to keep driving, **<u>no matter what.</u>**

3.   Remember to fuel your life and business when needed.

"Take your driver's license & learn the rules of the road. Now put some nice tunes on and steer towards the life of your dreams."
~ Gabriele Grikstaite

To successful "driving,"

Gabriele

About the Author

Gabriele Grikstaite, Cand.Merc., is a digital marketing and e-commerce consultant who lives in Copenhagen, Denmark. She loves helping creative individuals turn their passions into profits by helping them build profitable e-commerce businesses. It is her greatest pleasure to see new business owners reap the benefits of successful marketing and create the best possible future for themselves. Her methods have been designed based on ten-plus years of digital marketing experience and university studies at some of the world's most renowned business schools.

In her spare time, she loves going to the ice rink and rekindling her childhood passion: figure skating.

Gabriele Grikstaite

Contacts

Website: www.ecommercesuperpowers.com

Email: gaby@ecommercesuperpowers.com

LinkedIn: https://www.linkedin.com/in/gabrielegrikstaite

Facebook: https://www.facebook.com/gabriele.grikstaite

Instagram: https://www.instagram.com/gaby_grik

Learn how to double your e-commerce revenues in just three months without jeopardizing your marketing budget and maintain constant growth throughout the year:
https://www.ecommercesuperpowers.com/double-your-ecommerce-revenues

Nothing Matters Until You Matter

Jess Tayel
Business and Career Coach, Australia

"Change can be tough, but I've never heard anyone say it wasn't worth it."
~ Carol Dweck

At university, I promised myself I would not settle for the ordinary or the average, but I would strive to create value and a legacy. What I did not know back then was that I am going to face a few soul-sucking, energy-draining painful autoimmune diseases.

Every day was a struggle. Every day was different. Some were manageable; others were overwhelming. There were days when I could hardly even walk or stand up straight. Despite my illness, or perhaps because of it, I was able to build a successful international career and business as a business transformation consultant as well as a business and career coach. I have worked in over 11 countries, with over ten industries, delivering billions of dollars' worth of programs working for and with Fortune 500 companies, multinational organisations and courageous human beings.

In the years I spent climbing the corporate ladder and building my business, my illness hijacked my energy and vitality. My successful career journey had a parallel journey of figuring out what was wrong with me in addition to overcoming my physical and mental challenges

And then everything came crashing down on me with the unbearable pain that came after the loss of my only pregnancy. After over 20 years of struggle and a few surgeries, the struggle was given a name – a severe, rare and aggressive form of endometriosis. Finally, it all made sense.

After months of grief, reflection and acceptance, I came to believe that my curse was my blessing! I realised that my suffering had forced me to think, behave and learn differently. The need to find the shortest path to true success was my main driving force to do the deep inner work.

I did not have the energy to waste, and I would not let my dreams take ages to manifest. I wanted to spread my wings, and express who I am, do what I love and create my legacy.

I had to cut through the noise and see things for what they are, look at the big picture, connect the dots, and think holistically. I learnt to be self-aware, deliver with intention and adopt a learners' mindset.

It is critical to come from a place of inner power, to be at peace with my current situation and to strive to become better every day by embracing a growth mindset.

To know that I am not limited, that I can be more, do more and have more was vital to my success. It starts with knowing that you are whole and that you can change the way you see the world and how you interact with it, allowing opportunities to come your way and for everything to fall into place.

Self-perception

As a coach and a consultant, I consider myself a facilitator of change, a coach to my team, an advisor to my managers, and a partner to my colleagues. Acting from this position allows me to be more empathetic, look deeper, seek to understand first, and to create the right environment to enable the best value.

I see myself as a servant to my customers. Being a servant is being responsible, accountable and open to ideas and feedback. To be the guide who listens and implements. To do the right thing before doing things right and to establish value for the greater good.

My Values

I have always been determined to be true to myself. As I embarked on my career journey, I trusted that the universe would provide, would use me in the right place at the right time, and that when I am ready, things will fall into place.

This allowed me to let go, to be intentional, to work on my own terms, and according to my values. Some of the values I operate from are:

- Do what you love.

- Always aspire to create value.

- Success is to ensure that your customers get the service/product that makes their life easier.

- Budget entrusted to me = hardworking taxpayers' money. Always ask, is this the best use of their money?

- Perfection doesn't exist. There is only progress through the best you can.

- Be a caring and kind soul to others (seems like common sense, but it is something that I find to be lacking in some workplaces).

- Remember that people are the key to creating genuine, sustainable and adopted change.

- Stand for what is right and do everything possible to create an environment that is humane, just, and that fosters respect and appreciation.

- Accept obstacles as detours in the right direction, and that mistakes are a natural path to growth and learning.

- Always learn and master your practice.

My Career and Business

My work is so much more than a means of earning money. Don't get me wrong; money is essential and is one of the measurements of the value you bring to the workplace and clients, yet work means more to me. It is an expression of service, a way of being, my way of helping clients to solve problems, cultivate opportunities, and improve the lives of our customers.

Learning is a big part of my work. Not for certifications and titles, but to enrich the breadth and depth of my knowledge so I can put it all into practice. To create thought leadership, to practice critical thinking, to integrate different strategies and tactics, to focus on adding real value and introduce new ways of working gave me the agility to work in various capacities, solving a diverse set of problems with a variety of assignments, businesses and clients.

Here are some of my career and business views:

- Design your career, be intentional.

- Do not be the victim, seek to be the change.

- Be who **you** are and speak up.

- Show up, don't try to be perfect.

- Always introduce new ways of working and thinking.

- Simplify, do not complicate. To simplify is to be more empathetic and understanding of how to create sustainable change. Complexity is the enemy of execution and progress.

- Embrace constructive feedback.

- Build good relationships as a career and business currency.

- Remember that good quality time spent in understanding the problem and designing a solution is as important as the time spent in implementation and delivery.

- Be humble; clients need guides, not heroes.

- Leave toxic environments that are beyond fixing. (I know this can be controversial, yet based on my experience and that of my clients', working in a place that is not aligned with your values for too long will cause damage. Unfortunately, sometimes the damage is long-term or permanent.)

- Be flexible and openminded. Do not get addicted to being right.

My Mindset Foundations

I have learnt so many practices and tools over the years, but none of these would work if my mindset is not in the right place. I had my peaks and valleys, hard days and good days, times when self-doubt crawled in, moments of despair and giving up. I've been bullied, fired, put down, I've made bad decisions and trusted the wrong people. Yet, I am still here, I am successful and fulfilled in my career and business because of these foundations that helped me carry on.

Endurance is Key

I came to understand early in my career that I needed to endure.

The path to success and greatness is not easy; life throws so many curve balls at you. Nothing worth having is easy to come by. It is essential to focus on your inner powers rather than get attached to external outcomes and drivers.

For me, endurance was one foundational element to allow me to reach my goals.

Endurance is not bottling up things and trying to fit in to get by. On the contrary, this would be a passive rejection of life that generates negative energy and emotions which will come to haunt you later.

To endure is to have focus, to persevere, to know that you are part of something bigger, to see things through to the end and be congruent with your true self.

You don't need more strength to carry more baggage. Instead, carry less baggage, the right baggage.

Set Your Intention

I found that having an intention is like having a north star. Your identity, attitude and behaviour stem from your intention. It keeps you on the path and guides you when you stray. Your intention has to be explicit and clearly defined otherwise it won't be as binding.

Having a clear intention helped guide my decision-making process and gave grounds to my actions. As a result, my actions are intentional and not reactive.

Intention is attention, and where your intention flows, your life will follow.

Let Go and let In

To let go is to allow. To allow your purpose to flow through you, to let go of the need to have it your own way, to be right and to understand that you are part of a bigger scheme.

You are at your place of work to learn and teach, be open, leave a legacy, to make the place better than it was and to help others grow. Letting go does not mean taking the back seat; on the contrary, you do your best to do the right things the right way.

The opposite of this is to resist, to make assumptions, have a predetermined way of how things should be; they are only in it for themselves and their hidden agendas. This path only leads to putting others down, disregarding what is right for the team and the business, creating noise and bringing busyness. This kind of mindset creates stress that develops friction in the environment, waste everyone's time and energy, and brings about a sense of resentment.

"It is not life's events that are causing problems or stress. It is your resistance to life's events."
~ Michael A. Singer.

Becoming vs Having

From my experience in my career and coaching, I have seen many people work backwards when it comes to 'becoming vs having'. They want to have what makes them happy and fulfilled first before learning how to become the identity and character that allows those things to come their way.

To 'become' is to adopt the mentality, language and belief of what you aspire to be. It requires awareness, discipline, openness and flexibility.

This mindset aspect was the first that I adopted. I was always a keen observer of how people around me navigated towards success, how they spoke, what they read, their daily routine etc. Learning by observation has helped me to gain a few steps ahead.

"It is the close observation of little things which is the secret in business, in art, and in every pursuit of life."
~ Samuel Smiles

The Feel-good Trap

We are all addicted to feeling good, and there is nothing wrong with that. The question is, what triggers you to 'feel good'? This question is a deep one that needs to be carefully considered. In my coaching sessions, this question revealed many triggers, beliefs and values that control mindset and decision-making process.

One trap that I've seen some professionals fall into is to keep doing the same job for so many years though they had opportunities to progress elsewhere. I've witnessed this particularly in the contracting space where professionals keep getting the same job over and over again, solving the same set of problems, not growing their careers, and before you know it, many opportunities have passed by and its too late

Another trap that many, including myself, have fallen victim to is the addiction to being right. I've observed many follow this path and get rewarded for it! The need to be right carries so much resistance and force that it triggers a counterforce in the other party that you need to win over.

The need to be right has become an organisational pandemic that justifies the use of power, verbal abuse, unethical behaviour, losing sight of what is right and stepping over others. Unfortunately, the higher up you are in the corporate hierarchy, the more serious the impact is.

Once I realised how self-destructive this behaviour could be on my career and wellbeing, I made a conscious decision to let it go and persevere in making sure that I do not fall back into it.

"From a worldly point of view, there is no mistake so great as that of the being always right."
~Samuel Buttler

Dipping In and Out

There were many times when it was hard to stick to my growth mindset. Sometimes I would dip into the familiar fixed mindset. Then, sooner or later, I would realise what I'd done and to go back to reinforcing my growth mindset. My difficult health situation provided the incentive to grow and persevere.

This is a continuous learning process that requires being mindful, purposeful and open to changing your ways of thinking to get to the next milestone faster and better.

You've probably heard this before, but it's worth repeating: there is no failure, only learning. There is so much time that can be gained from not allowing mistakes or misjudgements to take hold over you. Instead of wasting time worrying about your mistakes, use that time to learn from them and continuously improve.

"Don't worry about failure. Worry about the chances you miss when you don't even try."
~ Sherman Finesilve

Emotions

One day I read a statement that had a profound effect on me, and I pledged to embrace it as much as I can:

"Feelings buried alive never die."
~ Karol K. Truman

Given my health situation, I had to maintain positive emotions that create a sense of contentedness, groundedness and hope.

Working on your mindset is very rewarding, but if you have negative emotions that are not dealt with, then over time, your efforts to build a growth mindset can be jeopardised.

"Negative emotions tend to facilitate a more Fixed Mindset. Mood and emotions are very interlinked with our mindsets."
~ Dr Ben Palmer, BAppSci (Hons) PhD, Chief Executive Officer, Genos International

Our ability to manage our emotions and have a healthy way of expressing them plays a huge role in our ability to grow and sustain a healthy mindset.

It was essential for me to have an outlet to express my emotions in my work environment and allow others to do the same. I found this to be one of the most challenging aspects to deal with. It is easy to claim that work and life are separate, but in reality, they are not.

Making the conscious decision to be aware of your emotions and their effect on how you show up in the world is critical to your success. Emotions are powerful, and they can quickly mask the progress that you have made on your mindset and hijack the show.

"Emotions can get in the way or get you on the way."
~ Mavis Mazhura

Putting the Power Back in Your Hands

"If you change the way you look at things; the things you look at change."
~ Wayne Dyer

In my 20-plus year of experience, I have witnessed many significant achievements and met and worked with exceptionally successful professionals. Yet unfortunately, there are also many professionals out there who are stuck.

These are some of the things my clients used to say:

"I am just in it for the money, I am stuck and can't find a way out of this job."

"I left corporate to run a business, and now I feel I need to go back to finding a job. Am not sure I can get this business to make money."

"I always wanted to be in a leadership role, but now I realise this is a equal to not having a life anymore."

"Big part of my leadership is ensuring everyone does the work; this is energy draining."

"Many opportunities passed me by because I just kept quiet."

"My team doesn't respect me, I know it, I feel it, and it makes me sad."

"If I continue to work like this, am going to get sick."

"I know I can do the job better than many people I met in higher places, but I can't seem to know how to sell my experience in a way that is articulate and appealing."

These are hardworking, high-performing good people who have reached their glass ceiling. I am grateful that I am able to help hundreds of clients around the world to overcome their self-doubt and lack of confidence to:

- Deliver successful world-class corporate programs;

- Have a sustainable, thriving and profitable business;

- Become a well-respected and sought after leader;

- Master their practice;

- Build robust and authentic personal brands;

- Build a growth mindset;

- Easily articulate and sell their expertise.

They can now spread their wings to create the change they always wanted to achieve – to realise their dreams, to have their confidence restored, to become happier, making the income they deserve and spending quality time with their families.

Change their reality from working crazy hours, feeling unfulfilled, missing on opportunities, managing a business that is haemorrhaging money and having to put up with jobs and companies that forces them to be fake to gain social acceptance.

They can now be their true authentic self and bring good into the world sooner rather than later.

"Remember, what you are not changing, you are choosing."

Read that again!

The Secret Sauce

It is now more than ever that the world needs meaningful change. I have reached my level of success in corporate and business by being **me**.

The fact of the matter is, there is no magic formula, grand certification or a magic wand! There is only **you**. You are the secret sauce. You are unique, capable, deserve better, and you matter. Your experiences, your culture, your values, your learnings, and your personality are all ingredients of this secret sauce, that is **you**.

You must take ownership, accept responsibility, and do the work on yourself.

What helped me develop my secret sauce was working with great coaches and leaders who inspired me, helped me realise my blind spots and challenged me to step outside my comfort zone.

"The power is within you. It always has been. How far are you willing to expand the horizons of your thinking and stir that power awake?"
~ Louise Hay

Success Actions

1. Be intentional and do the inner work every day. Do not be on autopilot.

2. Remember that simple is genius.

3. Never stay in a place that does not recognise your value

4. Work on you, for you, and everything else will fall into place.

5. Foster a more humane environment that cherishes differences and cultivates collective intelligence.

6. Design your career to serve you on your terms.

7. Embrace your uniqueness as your superpower.

8. Hire a coach if you want a shortcut to success; this has accelerated my growth and learning more than anything else.

9. Adopt a learner's mindset and keep an open mind to change.

10. Always smile in the face of adversity!

"You presume you are a small entity, but within you is enfolded the entire universe."
~ Ali ibn Abi Taleb

Jess Tayel

About the Author

Jess Tayel is a corporate business transformation consultant, an entrepreneur, a business coach and a career coach. Jess serves business owners as well as corporate leaders and professionals.

She helps businesses build striving, sustainable and profitable businesses by developing effective and efficient systems using business-driven processes that are managed by the right capable people to create sustainable change in an engaging environment.

Jess has helped business owners to build their businesses from strategy, sales, marketing, delivery, and customer services. She has also helped small and medium businesses to grow their profit to six and seven figures.

She also works with corporate professionals and leaders to break through their glass ceiling, fight the burnout, propel high performers to superior careers, build a world-class practice, and lead courageously.

She is obsessed with making careers and businesses fulfilling, a platform for self-expression, a place for delivering real value to customers, all while making high-level income/sustainable growing profit and never missing the right opportunities to grow and scale.

She has helped hundreds of business owners, senior corporate professionals and executive leaders in their businesses, careers, practice, mindset, and leadership.

Contacts

Business Name: WorkWorx & Business Made Successful

LinkedIn: www.linkedin.com/in/Business-Coach-Career-transformation-Leadership-Mentor

Book a call: https://calendly.com/jesstayel/virtual-coffee

Website: www.WorkWorx.com AND www.BusinessMadeSuccessful.com

WorkWorx Products and Services (For corporate leaders and professionals):

- **Corporate Leadership Mastermind:** High-level leadership mentoring program
- **Career Transition Mastery:** Transition to another branch of business transformation careers without starting from scratch
- **Coaching by Design membership:** 1:1 coaching membership program that covers a variety of topics and tailored to your needs
- **Career Accelerator Program:** Accelerate your progress from years to months
- **Mindset Impact Accelerator Program:** A Mindset focused 1:1 coaching program
- **Selling your expertise with stories:** Articulate your expertise into compelling stories that are on point, so you never miss an opportunity again or worse stay stuck in your current role

Business Made Successful Products and Services (For businesses):

- **Business Builder:** Working with business owners to build the business foundations
- **Business Scaler:** Scale your business and systems to the next level for higher profits
- **Profit Maximiser:** Business assessment and review to identify profit leakages areas and ways forward
- **Business Blackbelt:** High-level mastermind and group coaching for business owners
- **Operational Excellence:** A program that focuses on the business's core operations and systems to increase efficiency and throughput across all levels
- **Program Bullseye:** Not sure if your program will deliver to its promise, skeptical of the vendor's ability to deliver according to your expectations, not to their agenda, don't want to find out before it's too late, then Program Bullseye is here to ensure your success without the stress, overwhelm and excess time and budget.

From Breakdown to Breakthrough

Jessica Fox
Work-at-Home Empowerment Coach, USA

"Even your hardest circumstances can be your greatest teachers."
~ Jessica Fox

The Breakdown

I should have been enjoying an Easter feast with friends. Instead, I lay in a crumpled heap on my living room floor, bawling uncontrollably, while my husband stood by helpless and desperate for a solution. At that moment, no solution would come. All the pain, all the frustration, and all the disappointment came pouring out of me, sob after sob, as I rode out the most excruciating anxiety attack I have ever experienced. I finally hit the emotional, mental, physical, and spiritual wall I had been careening toward for years.

I would love to tell you that this was the moment that everything changed, but that wouldn't be the whole picture. I was "Superwoman," after all, and could figure this out on my own and pull myself up by my bootstraps. I was only tired, right? I figured a short, eight-week sabbatical should do the trick. The time off would help me rest and recuperate enough to get back to work and back to my normal life.

I couldn't have been more wrong.

I went back to work after my eight-week sabbatical, even though my head and heart were screaming for me not to, and this was when I began spiraling out of control.

I was easily angered and snapped at my spouse and children frequently. I was tired, and I needed daily naps to get through the day in one piece. I was emotionally unavailable to my young children and would often turn them away in anger and frustration, not angry with them but with myself as I had nothing left to give them. My work got every ounce of the focus, compassion, and energy I was able to give, and by the time I came home to my husband and kids, I didn't have a drop left. I began to turn inward, chastising myself for being a failure as a wife and emotionally berating myself for my inability to connect with my children. I just wanted the exhaustion and pain to end, but I felt totally trapped, believing I had no option but to try and get through the days. Those I turned to for help turned me away, and I continued to spiral down into a very dark place.

The Moment that Finally Changed Everything

I will never forget the look on my daughter's face – the fear, the shock, the betrayal, and the flood of tears. She was terrified as I erupted in a volcano of fury. To be honest, I don't even know what triggered the eruption, but I will never forget her look. The look in her four-year-old face made me run for my room, ashamed and guilt-ridden. This wasn't what I wanted for her, for my son, or my husband. This wasn't what I wanted for myself, and all I could think about was writing a letter to my husband and children about why their life was better off without me. I ended up crying myself to sleep that night while my husband soothed my daughter's fears and tears, and in the morning, he drove me straight to the doctor.

Merely ten weeks after I returned to work and in one quick swoop of my doctor's pen, my life was completely different. I was taken off work indefinitely and placed on disability – the diagnosis: major depression and burnout. My last ounce of will-power gave out that day, and my body collapsed – exhausted and defeated – as in a single moment, I lost everything. But, then and there, I started my journey back to health and the re-discovery of myself.

Our Reality

It's truly amazing how we, as women, can push ourselves and will ourselves to near-impossible lengths, ignoring the red flags and warning sirens going off in our hearts and minds. What troubles me is how hard we must fight to simply have dreams and passions and feel we are worthy to pursue them. It is also troubling how often we allow a sense of duty and obligation to completely override our inner wisdom and intuition, often taking us to the brink of mental, emotional, physical, and spiritual collapse.

Too many women, especially mothers, hold this inner tension between our dreams and sense of purpose and our perceived "duty" or role, be it in our work or as a spouse or mother. Too many of us believe that sacrificing our dreams and ambitions to motherhood is "the right thing to do." If and when we choose otherwise, we must prove our decision through our success, inevitably working ourselves to exhaustion. It seems that no matter what we choose, we receive condemning comments from societal trolls. We end up losing ourselves a little bit at a time, arriving in a place where we no longer recognize the hollow woman in the mirror.

Determined Decisions Change Circumstances

When I hit the brick wall of burnout, I was but a shell of the woman I once had been. Yet, when I look back on those long months of recovery, I am filled with gratitude because it was in those months, I learned who I truly was.

I made a decision, and I was determined to recover. I was determined to be better. I was determined to find my spark and passion again. It was in those moments I committed never to allow my outside circumstances to exert so much control over my life, my thoughts, and my feelings. I committed to being a present and connected mother, and I committed to figure out how I could find the sweet spot of a deep relationship with my family, while still pursuing my passions and dreams. One of the most valuable things I learned was to accept and trust my inner wisdom and intuition and not allow "duty" to override them. I removed myself from the tightrope of "dreams **or** motherhood," which is a common either/or complex in North America, and rest in my truth – I love being a mom, fullness of who I am is not expressed in motherhood. My purpose is greater than my motherhood, and it is 100% okay for me to pursue my passions and potential because not only am I happier – it makes me a **better** mom and spouse.

I would love to tell you these realizations happened overnight and that my recovery was easy – but that would be a lie. It took nearly two years for my strength to return and many hours of working with professionals to get my depression and anxiety under control. My lack of income had severe consequences on the financial stability of our family, and this led to near bankruptcy and moving nearly 2,000 miles to a new country (which is a story I will share in my next book), but this never quelled my determination to be **better**! I knew that **better** was possible, and every day, I stepped into that possibility, taking back responsibility and control for my own life and learning to be the creator of my circumstances rather than a victim to them.

We all have circumstances in our lives that are less than rainbows and daisies. We all have parts of ourselves and our story that we would like to hide or forget about. But my question for you is this: have you allowed yourself to learn and grow from the pain and hardship? Or have you allowed yourself to be victimized by it? Or perhaps still, you are somewhere in-between, as many of us find ourselves. No matter where you are on that spectrum, know that even your most challenging circumstances can be your greatest teacher.

My Hard-Knock Lessons to Live By

Want proof? Well, let me share with you some of the incredible lessons I am forever grateful for that came out of my season of burnout and recovery:

Lesson 1: Listen to Your Inner Voice & Intuition

When I reflect on the months and years leading up to my burnout, one thing that stands out is that I knew I was in the wrong job, but I let a false sense of duty and responsibility to the organization I was serving override what I knew was true: that the situation wasn't ideal for my unique personality and talents to truly shine.

Our intuition is there for a reason! It guides us towards the best and brightest version of ourselves and lets us know when something we think, feel, or do is out of alignment with our potential and purpose. Our inner voice deserves our respect, and when we listen, we will truly experience a full expression of ourselves in this world.

Lesson 2: Don't Neglect the Nurturing of Your Soul

<u>Self-care is non-negotiable!</u> Again! **<u>Self-care is non-negotiable!</u>** (Let me hear you in the back!) The most important resource you have **<u>is you!</u>** Invest your time and energy in the things that give you joy, that make you feel alive, and that help you feel rejuvenated. Whatever that looks like, set aside time every day for the care and nurture of your own soul. The level that you can show up in the world, fully sourced, is the level that you can best serve and impact the world around you.

Lesson 3: Determination and Commitment are a Power Couple

If you desire something in your life, be determined and committed to see it manifest. No matter what it is, the combination of determination and commitment (also known as **<u>faith</u>**) will bring about our expressed desire. Do not worry about how it will come about for the "how" is always revealed along the journey. Rather, stay focused on what it is you desire and why you desire it, determined and committed to see that happen, and it will come to pass in the perfect moment for your greatest benefit.

Lesson 4: Embrace Both/And

There is nothing wrong with wanting it all and going for it! For too long in our society, women have been told that that they should be content with motherhood and sacrifice themselves for family and children. They have silently condemned for seeking fulfillment "outside the home." First off, I say **Bullshit!** Why on earth should a woman sacrifice her personhood, her potential, and purpose just because she has children? Why should a woman be condemned for desiring more for herself than spit-up stains on her shirt and the never-ending gruel of cleaning up after a toddler-tornado?

What was the purpose of the suffrage and feminist movements that called for the equality of women to be realized in our society if we condone these beliefs that a woman "should just be content" when children enter the picture. Rather, I believe it is in our best interest as women to run together, encouraging one another to be the fullest expression of ourselves. Let us band together and express joy when a woman stands up, in all her glory, in all her perfect imperfection, in all her motherhood and all her passion, declaring "this is me!" and "I will live my life according to what pleases me!". It is time for our society to accept that women can be passionate and purposeful, while still being an incredible mother, whatever that looks like for her.

Lesson 5: What You Think, You Create

Whatever you choose to believe about yourself and your circumstance is true. If you believe it is a learning opportunity that can change your life for the better, it is. If you believe it is just evidence that nothing ever goes right and nothing will change, it is. For good or bad, what you think and what you put your mental energy towards will come to pass in your life. We always have a choice: Will I be a victim of my circumstance and perpetuate a victimized existence? Or will I put the power of my thoughts to work and create a better future for me to experience?

When we understand the reality of this statement, "What I think, I create," it puts into motion the desire for constructive, life-giving thinking that transforms our lives in remarkable ways.

Lesson 6: Own Your Truth

No matter what you choose or pursue in this life, let it be true to you, and don't let anyone tell you otherwise. Well-meaning people in our lives will counsel us in ways contrary to what we know is true for ourselves, and I implore you to have the fortitude to stay in alignment with what you know is right for you. This is why I started the <u>Thriving Work-at-Home Mama Movement</u> – a place for women who choose to grow a business from their home office while raising children.

For some of us, we desire to be home and available for our children, but still seek to express our professional creativity, independence, and savvy in entrepreneurial ways. We have chosen neither the path of the working mom or stay-at-home mom, but rather, we have chosen both and are forging our own way in beautiful chaos.

What is your truth? Discover it, own it and live it out loud!

My Breakthrough

The lessons I learned in the burnout and recovery season of my life have made me stronger and more tenacious than I have ever been. They have also lit a fire in me to be a light in the lives of other women who also desire to have it all, so they can do it without burning out as well. I now know my purpose is to empower women to realize their purpose, power, and potential, and I get to live this out every single day by helping others to thrive by coaching through my signature *Four Cornerstones Framework*.

I particularly love working with women who have chosen to work from home. The mission of the <u>Thriving Work-at-Home Mama Movement</u> is very simple: **<u>Work-at-Home Moms, Fully Supported!</u>** This dream is not just for this generation of mothers, but to release the next generation of mothers into their fullness along with future generations to come.

I've seen hundreds of women embrace their dreams and thrive successfully and confidently in both their business and motherhood, and as we continue in this season of COVID-19 and quarantine, thriving as a work-at-home parent has become crucial for the health of ourselves, our families, and our future. I've been able to rapidly grow my business, Jessica Fox Coaching, in the midst of fear and an economic downturn because I know the power of belief and that I am the creator of my circumstance. The best part is that I get to show others to do likewise.

As a result, I have booked virtual speaking gigs, podcasts, and interviews from women and organizations all around the world, and I am even being featured on *TED-Ed* in the fall of 2020.

My dreams are coming true, all while raising three children under seven years old, while homeschooling, and while being the best coach and entrepreneur I can be – and **<u>So Can You!</u>**

Takeaway Summary

So, to recap some key takeaways this chapter:

1. What did I choose to embrace that made me a better spouse and mother?

2. Fill in the blank: Self-care is ____________________!

3. Why is the power of belief crucial to our success?

Take Inspired Action

Here are three action steps you can take to facilitate a breakthrough in your life:

1. **Know Thyself!** Write out what you believe you have been placed on this earth to do. Don't know it? Think about the things that you love, that you enjoy, that you are talented at, and that give you energy. Things that people have pointed out as a gift they see in you. Compile these thoughts and ideas and allow a statement of purpose to come to the surface and then **own it!**

2. **Form the habit** of daily visualizing your desires. Invest time every single day and envision yourself experiencing the life that you desire. Allow yourself to feel, taste, see, smell, and touch that which you desire. Feel the joy and excitement of experiencing everything you want, and do this daily until it comes to pass.

3. **Hire a coach**. Invest in the support, the system, and the accountability that will help you go from where you are now to where you want to be, faster than you could ever think possible. Allowing ourselves to be coached creates rapid transformation and accelerates our breakthrough to success.

*"Find your alignment. Nurture yourself well.
Be the master of your circumstance. Build unstoppable momentum."*
~ Jessica Fox

Mama, **<u>You got this!</u>**

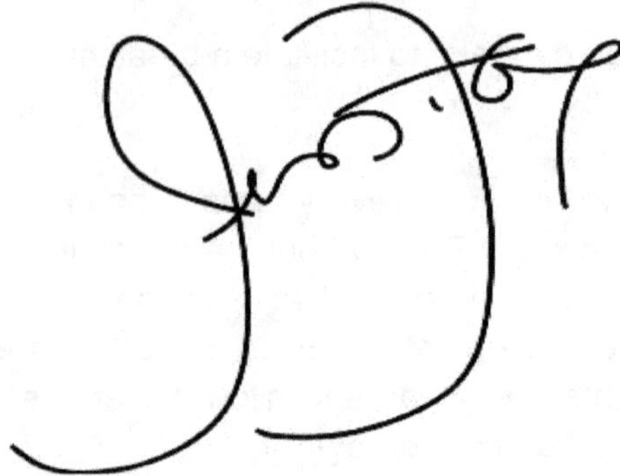

Jessica Fox

About the Author

My name is **Jessica Fox,** and I am passionate about helping women to fully realize their purpose, power, and potential. My mission is simple: <u>**Work-at-Home Moms, Fully Supported!**</u>

I'm a wife of one, mama of three, and a Work-at-Home Empowerment coach. I help work-at-home moms go from surviving to thriving! I have helped hundreds of women become confident that they can be successful in their career/ business **<u>and</u>** at being a great mom!

Most days, you will find me in my comfiest jeans, attempting to accomplish something work-related amid the chaotic hum of life with a young family, including a dog. I am a lover of musicals, *Harry Potter*, good coffee, and Jesus, and it isn't uncommon to find me lost in the woods or lost in my never-satisfied book addiction.

It is my joy and pleasure to inspire and journey with you, and others like you, as you say **<u>"Yes!"</u>** to yourself, **<u>"Yes!"</u>** to your dreams and desires, and **<u>"Yes!"</u>** to pursuing your future, fully supported.

Find Me

Receive your Free Time Mastery Gift:
https://bit.ly/timemasteryfreebie

More Great Gifts (Including the Work-at-Home Survival Challenge) at:
www.jessicafox.ca

Facebook: https://bit.ly/thrivingWAHMs

LinkedIn: www.linkedin.com/in/jessicafoxcoaching

Instagram: https://www.instagram.com/jessicafoxcoaching/

Email: jessicafoxcoaching@gmail.com

Confidence Coaching Works!

Linda Buchanan
Life Reset Rapid Transformational Therapy Practitioner (RTTP) and Life Coach, USA

"Coaching is winning – only faster!"
~ Linda Buchanan

The Meltdown

In my early thirties, the retail store I managed was a well-oiled machine with every cylinder firing. We worked our system every day and we enjoyed the spoils of our labors. It was so much **fun**!

Inconsistency existed within the district and the company for that matter, so many locations suffered trying to meet even the minimum sales requirements set forth by the company, as is unfortunately common in many national sales teams.

One day I received a corporate email that the regional manager in my area was no longer with the company. It was no surprise as that manager was moving to a location outside the company's scope. There was no announcement regarding a replacement or even an interim, which was odd. Only because the company was primarily run at the corporate level by military veterans, who seemed to operate under the mode to always have multiple backup plans.

Now to make things even more interesting, the CEO of our company travelled to my store, unannounced, later that same day with his entourage. The door beeps, I immediately head that way with a smile and a greeting to meet, the man I would learn very quickly was, the CEO! Pleasantly surprised, but not unprepared.

The CEO wanted to talk in my office after a quick tour of the store. He asked really good questions and, better yet, was interested in the answers. He was different. Inquisitive. He had 'looked under the hood and kicked the tires' and saw that everything was as it should be. There was nothing stashed, hidden or out of place. He wanted me to answer what I suspect he already knew to be true... did I have a system?

And if I did, could it be extrapolated across the retail division for the benefit of the entire company?

He didn't want me to just provide an answer. He wanted to KNOW the answer for himself. Then, he made me an unexpected offer.

The Offer: Go to another state and be the interim regional manager over four retail stores that were regularly underperforming and bring each of these stores to minimum expectations. All four stores at or above 100% for three consecutive months. I was given complete autonomy to hire/fire as needed and was provided a name that I would liaison with at corporate for reporting and communication during this time.

I could stay in the company owned apartment rent free during this three-month period. I would be paid as a regional manager during this interim period. That's all the instruction and concession I was provided.

This is when I learned that Yes, corporations do sometimes make out-of-the-box offers!

I was never asked how I would do it, or if I could do it, or if I thought I could do it. There was confidence implied in the question. Confidence that made me think... it might be possible.

The Bait/Bonus: If I successfully accomplished this goal of bringing these four underperforming stores up to the minimum expectation of 100% for three consecutive months, creating a habit of success... I would become the next regional manager. I would lead a three-state territory with 17+ stores.

The CEO had my attention.

My thoughts started racing as if he had pulled a chain in my mind. I had been in this store for almost a year and a half and it had taken well over three months to figure things out, iron out all the wrinkles, hire and then train the best people.

Was it even possible to turn four stores around in less than 30 days to meet the challenge and then maintain the momentum for the full 90 days with a team I had never even met?

I didn't know.

The Turning Point

The CEO gave me a couple of days to give him an answer... Yes or No. Then he said he would give me the rest of the week to get my 'house in order'... setting up my store and my home to be without me for the next three months. Then he and his entourage were gone.

I called my husband to tell him what happened. Once I knew that I had his support, I felt like I could breathe again! He knew we would have to figure some things out with 3 young kids, but my husband was the oldest of twelve kids so he had a lot of experience taking care of little ones. And I remember thinking… this could really be happening.

Then I shared the proposal with my team. Of course, they were all in!! Every employee in my store was fully capable of being interim manager while I was gone, but I could only choose one. I knew which of the reps wanted to advance into management based on our coaching conversations, which made the decision easy.

With an interim store manager in place, the decision was made to go and I would accept my fate whatever may come.

The Impact

I decided to go to the top performing store first. Thinking maybe they would just need a few tweaks to get above 100% to quota. If I could get that store up to speed within a few days, then it would be a success story that might be useful in helping the other three stores follow suit and build momentum quickly.

For the first full day at each location, I watched, listened and observed from the moment the first employee showed up until the last employee left. I watched them handle opening procedures, slow periods, peak times, incoming customer calls, inventory procedures, breaks/lunches, customer follow up calls, money procedures, clean up duties, closing procedures... all of it.

I had one-on-one sessions with each employee including the managers to get a feel for them as a person, gain perspective on their learning style, find out if they had any grievances that might hold them back in their performance, hear about their personal life and their personal goals and how the position they were in might help them achieve those goals, how they assessed their manager and what (if anything) they wished was handled differently by the manager, asked how long they had been with the company, what was their best customer experience, what was their worst, what did their significant other think of their job/their hours/their income, discussed babysitting issues around working a retail job, etc.

I learned everything I could about how the job was affecting their overall quality of life. I also reviewed their numbers with them for the past month/past quarter/past year and had them walk me through their numbers from their perspective about what challenges they perceived, how they were interpreting the data and what it was saying about them. Each of them said they had never considered that their sales numbers told a story about THEM as a rep.

One-on-one sessions are always fascinating and highly insightful!

The Truth Will Set You Free

In meeting with each employee, I also determined the level of desire each person had to improve, assessed strengths being underutilized by the team, where there might be opportunities for training and growth to impact the stores bottom line immediately, and how their current position might help fuel their goals and ambitions both personally and professionally. This was mission critical.

With only days to turn things around, there wasn't time to do job fairs, big hiring sprees, get new people trained up and still hit numbers for the current month! The CEO knew that and I knew that, though it had been unspoken. It was in everyone's best interest to re-train them rather than to start from scratch with new people.

I knew I had to be 1000% committed to the growth and success of these employees, and I learned very quickly that commitment made all the difference. This required a "burn the boats" mindset, which meant the only way out was forward! So my process became assess, train, coach and then re-assess.

Day Two through Day Ninety, we trained and implemented. I spent time explaining the 'why' for each part of their job and how everything they did or didn't do affected the clients and the end-of-month numbers, including the customer service reps. Customer service can make or break a business.

One of the most powerful insights this experience taught me was to always look for opportunities to give my employees, and customers alike, reasons to keep engaging. Positive coaching became critical for long-term growth and success.

The Ordinary World

Above all during these employee coaching assessments, I learned how each person wanted to be motivated to excel. For each person it can be a bit different - some love time-off, some love more money, some love free stuff, some love winning a contest. It was a game changer in terms of learning exactly how to motivate these folks to excel within their respective roles.

Personally, I love a combination of motivators… who doesn't love a buffet approach to winning with prizes, extra cash, time-off with loved ones, vacations and free stuff?!

Reaching deeper… it hit home with me on a profound level of how to motivate myself to get beyond what I believed might be possible in any given moment. This became an invaluable asset for me to know and understand, in terms of how to motivate myself to take decisive actions now.

I realized that I enjoy sales and coaching because at my core, I love making people happy. I was raised to be a people-pleaser and I'm glad! I enjoy seeing people smile and knowing I had a part in making that happen. It's a very powerful emotion for me and I find it deeply satisfying even now as a Confidence Coach.

Key Lessons and Words of Wisdom

It's beneficial to help yourself and your employees understand "why" you do what you do. It always matters to help folks see the big picture with respect to their individual contribution within their scope, how to increase their monthly income based on performance goals (sales, etc.), and how their contribution affects the overall team and/or company's performance goals. It's all interconnected.

I've adopted the phrase "looking down from 30,000 feet." I use it with clients often to put them in a position of power and control to look down and see the issue without attachment or judgment. Love this approach! Clients understand it and use it to resolve so many challenges that previously felt too overwhelming. It allows for perspective, and perspective leads to brilliance.

I use perspective in helping clients understand their value, gain confidence, and understand how it might help them to make their life better, easier, more comfortable, less stressed and/or more efficient. Confidence Coaching works!

Everyone had been trained and now they were implementing strategy. The managers delivered consistently stellar results as they now understood how to best manage their teams and their stores overall. These teams raved about each other, cheered each other on with every win, and enjoyed working together. Team spirit soared and so did the sales and profits!

I found lots of gems in each store with different personalities and strengths within each team. Something incredible happened. The first store started to become a resource for the second store, and the first and second store started to become a resource for the third store, and so forth. We had created a true network that was strong and integrated for support, consistency and comradery. Training and communication were on point.

The store managers suddenly had an extra 22+ hours a week freed up from inventory and customer service tasks that took them from 70+ hours a week to about 48-52 hours a week. BOOM!!

And just like that, life became more **fun**!

Stores generated more than double the revenue, store assets were protected, customers were raving, and reps began talking about their futures within the company. Amazing!

These are the lessons I learned on my path to success in the corporate realm as a manager, a coach, a cheerleader, a trainer and a leader:

Wisdom #1 – When it comes to business, even marketing, operate with multiple backup plans. This is one of the best strategies for success in business, and I have been blessed in my private coaching practice because of my willingness to be flexible and have contingency plans.

Wisdom #2 – Run my business in such a way that **anyone** could walk in at any time. If I'm doing things right, then any pop-in visit will be a bright spot in my day.

Wisdom #3 – The customer absolutely deserves to have the best experience. Always!

Wisdom #4 – Cross-train to prepare people to move up in business and in Life. Allow them to carry your legacy forward.

Wisdom #5 – Never ask anyone to do anything you're not willing to do yourself. You may choose not to do it as the best use of your time, but willingness is everything.

Wisdom #6 – If I want different/better results, I need to do things differently. Be open to change and adapt to get your best results!

Wisdom #7 – It always pays to invest in myself and my people, even if I suspect they will move on... because many do move on, and that's okay. I want to work with ambitious and driven people!

Wisdom #8 – Know myself and know my employee and my customer avatars. Sometimes we are one and the same. Other times, not so much.

Wisdom #9 – People will do what they understand and will choose not to do anything they don't understand. Clarity is everything… in sales, in coaching and in Life.

The Reward

It was done.

I had successfully duplicated my store into four more equally successful stores. By the end of the 90 days, these stores were all experiencing HUGE financial gains, strong team comradery, and were exceeding their monthly quotas by 200%+ month after month.

Each team member now had a clear vision and goal that wasn't just dictated by the company parameters but had evolved into something **bigger**. Each person demanded MORE of themselves. The money was flowing and life was good!

These amazingly talented folks just needed someone to open them up to a different way and that's what coaching is all about! Coaching really is about helping folks just like me get where we want to go faster and easier than we ever thought possible. Confidence Coaching works!

Together, we created an alternate, much more successful reality. I use these same strategies and methods, along with an entire toolbox of new techniques, to help my coaching clients to achieve huge wins to get the dream life they want to start flowing with ease.

Coaching and mindset is everything in achieving success in this life. In the corporate world, the company often picks up the tab. But for me (and so many others), I had to choose to invest in myself, my own healing and rapid transformations. I had to create my own environment for breakthroughs, growth and paradigm shifts.

I bought "all the best and most touted" books, and then devoured them. I made the lessons apply to my life. I took course after course after course, and I found my own coaches and mentors to help me work through various issues that might otherwise hold me back in my personal and professional life. I don't allow them to fester for any length of time. I nip things immediately and keep moving forward!

Things I Couldn't Figure Out Quickly for Free

Now I choose to invest well in paid coaches that allow me and my business to grow even **faster**! There's a powerful Energy connection in an exchange of money for services that I had never understood previously. All of it… the law of attraction, the law of polarity… it all existed. Once I learned that, I could never go back! It's weird even to me after all this time, the more I pay and commit… the deeper my transformation. It's incredible!

I even became a certified Rapid Transformational Therapy Practitioner (RTTP) and Life Coach to help my clients and myself even more! Learning all of this myself took time, money and resources. If I could have hired a coach originally, it would have been more affordable and I would have achieved amazing results so much faster.

I had to face my shortcomings head on, and do the work to heal, often alone. It was hard and took so much time on my own. With what I've learned, now my clients get results **fast** and **permanently**.

Great coaching gave me so many possibilities! Now I get to work with hundreds of clients who understand the power and speed of Confidence Coaching to get them to the top of their game… and keep them there.

Power Summary

Let's recap some of the key points of this chapter:

1. Fill in the blank. Look down from ___________ feet to see the big picture to make pivots from a place of power and control.

2. What was the key lesson that I learned when I chose to see people as talented and worthy of re-training, instead of broken and dismissive?

3. What was the impact on my business when I chose Confidence Coaching to **win**?

Success Actions

Confidence Coaching allows you to experience the most positive moments with other people as you learn to love yourself and others in the best, most powerful and meaningful ways.

Here are three success actions to increase your own personal level of success:

1. Make a list. Decide what's most important in your life, write it down and start opening your mind to the thought that everything you want is possible.

2. Create a mantra for success, such as "I am amazing and create my own destiny." Then post it on your mirrors, your fridge, your planner, your computers, your TV, your phone screens and even in your vehicle.

3. Hire an amazing Coach to get THE WIN faster and better than you ever thought possible! Stop leaving your success to chance. Collapse time on your goals for the win and enjoy more money, more time, more freedom, more romance, more connection and more adventure NOW.

"Collapse time on your goals with Confidence Coaching and start living your best life today! Don't wait because your amazing life is only 90 days away."
~Linda Buchanan

So Much Love and the Brightest of Blessings,

Linda

About the Author

Linda Buchanan is a Rapid Transformational Hypnotherapy Practitioner (RTTP) and Life Coach who lives in the U.S.A. with her husband of 25+ years. Linda is a proud momma of three grown children and their significant others. She loves being a Grandma to the most adorable little helpers. She has served her Heavenly Father and Jesus Christ faithfully for 17+ years and celebrates members of all faiths.

She loves freeing people from limiting beliefs and/or phobias with RTT and then coaching them to their Bliss Point to live the life they truly desire **now**!

Linda chose Rapid Transformational Therapy with over a 30-year track record to get quick, effective and permanent results that clients actually want. She works online with clients from over five continents. Clients find RTTP Coaching a worthy investment as they get exactly what they want – freedom from the painful problems of their past and clarity for a bright future. It is her calling and her passion.

Contacts

Website: https://www.liferesetfast.com

Email: liferesetcustomerservice@outlook.com

Facebook: http://www.facebook.com/lindamariebuchanan

LinkedIn:
https://www.linkedin.com/in/linda-buchanan-328a0826

Twitter: @LindaBWorks

Instagram: https://www.instagram.com/emeraldzanddiamondz/

Being Unstoppable

Michael Armstrong
Entrepreneur, USA

"The only true handicap anyone has is the lack of belief in oneself!"
~ Shihan Michael Armstrong

The Sacrifice

Have you ever thought about what you would be willing to do for your life's passion? As a serious martial artist, I freely gave of my time, money, and multiple injuries to the development of my art. However, "What are you willing to sacrifice?" is the question I had to answer at the age of 22. I had been in the martial arts for 11 years when a doctor told me that I would have to quit karate or go **blind**. I attempted to give up on this part of my life, but after much deliberation, I decided that I could not forgo this fundamental piece of who I had become!

I have had vision problems since birth, and like many people, I had to wear corrective lenses. Then when I was 16, I tore my retina due to a hit on the head. After seeing several doctors, I was diagnosed with a disease that made my eyes more susceptible to retinal detachments. No surgery was necessary at that time, and the only recommendation was to put an extra pillow under my head when I slept. This scenario repeated itself three more times, until at 22 when I was told that they could not save the vision in my right eye. The doctor also informed me that I had to "…quit doing all contact sports, including martial arts, or you will go blind."

Can you imagine being 22, a 2nd-degree blackbelt, having karate students, and a very active lifestyle and having to quit? I tried. For three months, I stopped training and teaching. This put me into a state of depression. I decided that I could not live my life in a constant state of fear of what could happen. So, I started my classes back up and continued my studies. At first, I did not spar or take any falls, but with time I gradually incorporated them back into my life. This may have led to my downfall.

The Downfall

It was a Tuesday morning when it was made quite apparent to me that I could no longer ignore my vision issue. I was driving to my job at Home Depot when my lack of sight nearly cost me my life. I had already gone blind in my right eye, and I was starting to have some problems with my left. It was becoming very sensitive to light, making it extremely difficult for me to keep it open. I already had the darkest tint on my Toyota 4x4's windows, as well as a set of sunglasses over my prescription glasses. This helped, but not enough. The sunlight was quite literally painful on my "good" eye. At the time, I knew with the pain and headaches I was experiencing that I should get in to see a doctor, but I always found a reason to put it off.

This particular morning, I was driving down Greenway Road on my way to work and having a hard time keeping my left eye open. The sun was bothering my eye much more than usual. It was tearing up, and it was a challenge just to keep my eye open and in focus. Greenway is an extremely busy road in Phoenix, and it is not a good road to have one's eyes closed. It is a miracle that I am still alive. As I was coming up on Seventh Street, I could barely keep my eye open, and I did not see the light. There were no cars in front of me as I approached the intersection. I guessed at the time the light was green. Well, it wasn't. As I flew through the light, I saw that it was red. My heart jumped into my throat.

As I passed the light, I saw two cars slide by in my rear-view mirror, just missing me. I knew that I could no longer put off seeing a doctor. Later that day, I called a retinal surgeon and set up an appointment for the next day.

I remember driving into the doctor's parking lot and just sitting in my truck, fearing what I might find out. My experience with eye doctors in the past was not very positive. It was just four years prior that I went to a retinal specialist for my right eye, but unfortunately, they were not able to save the sight in the eye. My eye ended up with a severe retinal tear, which became infected and induced glaucoma. I hoped sincerely that this time would be different.

The Surgery

My first impression of Dr. Smith was really good. He was around fifty with a slightly husky build. He was balding with a friendly and confident smile. He started off with, "Hello, Mike, I am Dr. Smith. Why don't you sit down and tell me exactly what is going on with your eyes?" he added.

"Thanks, Doc. I will," I said as I sat down.

I then went on to tell him how I had extreme sensitivity to light. I also informed him that I was experiencing quite a bit of pain in both eyes. "Well, let's take a look at your good eye first," he said as he dimmed the lights. After a thorough examination, Dr. Smith informed me that I had a cataract on my eye, and that was what was causing my light sensitivity.

He also found a retinal tear. "Mike, I must say this is very serious. If you do not have surgery to correct this problem, you will go blind within the next five years. This is my specialty, and I have a success rate of ninety percent," he said. He recommended that I go to another retinal clinic for a second opinion, so I did. They gave me the same diagnosis and recommendation. It did not take me long to decide to have the procedure done. We set the surgery for three days later.

My family, friends, and girlfriend were shocked by the news, but very supportive. My band members were like brothers to me and let me know that no matter what happened, we would work it out. I believe that we all felt that the surgery would be successful, and life would go on as normal. The odds were in my favor, but I had reservations. The next three days were like torture. Not knowing what or how my life could change was unbelievably difficult. Questions like; *Did I pick the right doctor?, Should I do this now?, Am I going to go blind?* made it nearly impossible for me to focus on anything other than my upcoming surgery.

The Last Sunset

I cannot remember what exactly motivated me to go outside the night before my procedure, but I thank God for that insight. It was around five in the afternoon when I drifted outside. I recall looking at the sky and wondering what it would be like to never see such beauty again. Feeling foolish, I started to head back into the house. Then it really set in that I might never see another sunset again. I immediately stopped and made watching the Arizona sunset my priority.

If you have never seen an Arizona sunset, it is something truly amazing. The colors I saw that night are still vivid in my mind today. As the Sun moved through the sky, blue gradually turned to violet. The Sun's rays shifted from gold to orange bursting through the few clouds like spotlights. Slowly, the sky turned from an intense crimson to a brilliant purple, finally fading to evening's black. As I watched the stars come out, my eyes teared up, and I prayed that I would see such beauty again. Unfortunately, this was not to be. That was the last sunset I ever saw.

The Turning Point

Blindness is the most difficult thing I have ever had to deal with. I knew I did not want to wallow in self-pity, so I immediately decided to move on with my life. My family, sensei, students, friends, and government were very supportive. I think this: my faith and the discipline of the martial arts were instrumental in making my transition relatively smooth.

Within three weeks of my final eye surgery, I was enrolled in the vocational rehab program for the blind. I figured that learning blind skills was just a matter of understanding the techniques to accomplish the task. As I went through the different subjects, I felt like the knowledge was giving me my independence and freedom back. I learned how to safely walk with a cane. Then, understanding the basics of activities of daily living taught me about how to cook, clean, and organize everything from my food to my mail.

When I learned how to read Braille, labeling and keeping things organized became much easier. Technology was far from what it is today, but learning how to use a computer opened an entire world of possibilities. Now with the advances of our cellphones, the world has never been as accessible as it is today.

After completing my blindness training, I became involved with the Foundation for Blind Children. Through giving back to this beautiful cause, I felt an incredible sense of satisfaction. They had me teach their children and adult clients about both fitness and self-defense. This led to me getting involved in several events to raise funds and awareness for this incredible organization. Interestingly enough, the first of which I was one of eight blind hikers that climbed to the top of Mount Kilimanjaro in June of 2009.

This event started me on a journey of several challenging adventures including a hike to the base camp of Mount Everest and a 57-day hike of the 807-mile Arizona Trail.

In many ways, my abilities as a teacher and a practitioner of the martial arts has improved exponentially after blindness. I have been able to dedicate more time to improve my teaching and expand my training. I have now been a sensei for nearly thirty years, and the challenges derived from blindness have helped drive me to be the best martial artist I can be.

To this end, I have cross-trained in multiple forms of martial arts. I have a sixth-degree black belt in Kyokushin Karate, and it is and always will be my first love. I have earned a third-degree black belt in jujitsu and a black belt in traditional Samurai Sword. In all, I have trained in over ten different martial arts and am still training and learning new material.

My dedication to the martial arts did not go unnoticed. I have been inducted into the Martial Arts Masters Hall of Fame and received several awards for my devotion to growing my knowledge and understanding of the martial arts.

The Growth

Most people I meet have a hard time imagining how a blind man can teach martial arts. However, I have adapted and am now quite adept at it. In fact, there have been several instances where visitors have observed an entire class without realizing that I am blind.

When I teach, I use spatial awareness in conjunction with such things as being aware of sounds as subtle as cloth rubbing or a foot adjustment to lock in on where a student is and how they are standing. The two things I have to pay close attention to is articulation when verbalizing techniques and solid representation when demonstrating. I also take full advantage of my sensei or students' sight to help me correct mistakes I may miss. My students are progressing quite well and seem very happy with their training.

As a blind man, I have not fully mastered the blocking of punches or kicks yet, but this ability is getting better every day. I had one student that worked with me for six months until she finally approached me and said she knew I had to see a little bit. I laughed and proceeded to show her that my eyes were both prosthetic and came out. To say the least, she was very surprised.

There are methods from all over Asia that teach how to heighten your senses to incredible levels, and I have trained in systems from both Korea and Indonesia that help with this. I am currently training in the Indonesian martial art system Merpati Putih to this end. I still believe that Kyokushin and Aiki Jujitsu is the ideal combination of systems for the blind. Kyokushin is perfect because of the conditioning and the aggressive nature of our fighting. Aiki Jujitsu is also excellent because of its hands-on approach to self-defense and ground fighting.

The Wisdom And Lessons

Wisdom #1 – Be Open and Willing

The martial arts taught me that anything can be accomplished if you are willing to do the hard work and open to learning. Far too often, we can't let go of our knowingness or ego to be open to accept knowledge.

Wisdom #2 – Don't Give Up

As a master martial artist, I can tell you to not give up! You may have to flow around or redirect a problem, but always keep your final goal in mind.

Wisdom #3 – The Power of the Mind

Remember that the most powerful weapon anyone has is their mind. Visualizing your goals and understanding that one is always a student will give you endless possibilities.

The Reward

There is no way to know if karate was the cause of my blindness, but I know the martial arts and going blind have given me insight and the tools to succeed at anything I put my mind to.

These life lessons have helped me become an entrepreneur, professional speaker, author, life coach, and sensei. Teaching and sharing what I have learned has improved my quality of life a thousand-fold. The love of my life, my wife, was one of my students, and many of my best friends are martial artists.

My life is good, and only getting better. Often, people ask me, "How does a blind man do all these amazing, crazy things?"

I reply, "The only real handicaps any of us have is the lack of belief in our self and the strength of mind/will to circumvent or overcome the obstacles life throws at us!"

If you are willing to do the work to change your mindset and stay true to your goals, the possibilities are boundless!

Shihan Michael Armstrong

"Life is all about growth, and the key to growth is being open-minded as a student in all things!"
~ Shihan Michael Armstrong

Power Summary

Let's summarize this chapter and power through the key lessons:

1. Life challenges can be of incredible leverage for drive and success.

2. Anything can be overcome with the proper mindset

3. Always strive to learn and grow

Success actions

Here are three actions that you can take to help you move forward in life:

1. Find something to change your state of mind when a negative thought comes in. Examples are dancing, watching a movie, movement, breathing, walking, etc.

2. Find the training method that gives you the outcome that you're looking for. An example is if you want to be a public speaker, find a program that is going to give you the tools that you need to give you the speaking ability

3. Take the time to practice speaking your unique heroic identity so that it becomes natural for you.

About the Author

Shihan Michael Armstrong is an entrepreneur, professional speaker, life coach, and author. He has been featured in *USA Today*, *The Today Show*, *Arizona Highways*, and several news programs, both local and national. In spite of being totally blind, he has traveled the world climbing mountains like Kilimanjaro and Mount Everest Base Camp. He has raised nearly $1 million for causes around helping blind children and adults experience a higher quality of life. He is dedicated to helping the world realize their full health potential and how it affects every aspect of who they are.

Michael and his wife Tiffany host a show and have a coaching platform to help inspire people to have more success and joy. Their show, *United Through Vision,* focuses on sharing stories of heart-centered people that want to make the world a better place. They hope to inspire and help people realize that vision is from the heart and not from the eyes.

Core causes are health and wellness, breaking down barriers around handicaps, and helping people realize that we are all connected.

Contacts

Facebook: Whole Body and Mind Wellness

YouTube: United Through Vision, Whole Body and Mind Wellness

Books to be released next year are:
- *Whole Body and Mind Wellness*

- *Vision Beyond Sight*

Email: unitedthroughvision@gmail.com

From an Ugly Duckling to a Beautiful Swan

Najmunnisa Abdul Kader
Women's Voice Catalyst, Singapore

'Her shining eyes, revealing a world of lies. Wishing she could be a game-changer. Looking for a transformational charger. Finally, the road to freedom is unleashed. To shine her soul message! To inspire the masses with her mess! It is a divine message she believes! To show the world the celebrity newly conceived!'
~Najmunnisa Abdul Kader

Healing and forgiving oneself and others do not come overnight. God Almighty, through His mercy and guidance, sends transformational angels in the guise of awakened human beings. This, in turn, gives us the clarity to turn around ugly and untrue, old, negative conditionings. It gives us the impetus to bloom into the beautiful souls that we are in our natural and original state of being. Often years of negative conditioning and limiting beliefs are thwarted and newfound energy bursts open as a result of these transformations. It makes us feel weightless and able to radiate our light and greatness to the world.

My transformational story begins with my labelling myself as the 'Ugly Duckling'. Most of us are familiar with the famous childhood tale of the ugly duckling by Hans Christian Andersen, in which the duckling eventually turns into a graceful and beautiful swan. In a similar way, the image of the ugly duckling suited my inferiority complex and not feeling physically beautiful. In fact, I was nicknamed the 'Ugly Duckling' by my siblings. This story very much resonates with my childhood conditioning.

When I started my career in teaching some twenty years ago, I still held on to the belief that I was an ugly duckling. But just like the ugly duckling, I knew I possessed some strengths. I was exceptionally well versed in English and my mother tongue, Tamil. I had a mission to mould young minds. Yet over five years or so, my passion and mission went out of sight. I began to lose sight of the shore and fell into an abyss of depression and burnout. I suddenly was not the 'Sunshine' my colleagues in school had affectionately called me.

As time went on, I began to loathe my teaching career, but I still held onto the job because of financial commitments, and the job paid well. Also, at forty-six years of age, I believed it was difficult to change careers and start all over again. I was feeling stuck and lethargic.

I first took small, little, baby steps to reclaim my self-esteem by doing heart-centre meditation and breathing exercises. Every day I meditated for about twenty minutes by focusing on my heart. I also did deep breathing exercises that helped me clear my mind of clutter and helped me to be confident in myself. Like a rainbow appearing after a storm, I found the gifts with which I was born to serve with when I decided to attend a soul-transforming program. The course was from April 24th to April 26th in 2015 and ran for a full three days.

Since then, I have been practising forgiving myself and reaffirming myself that I am a beautiful soul with a loving and forgiving heart. My goal was to remove self-sabotaging beliefs that blocked me from realizing my true potential and the beautiful soul I was created to be from birth. I gave myself permission and approval to be the graceful swan I had been, in essence, all along. I was ready to shed the damaging image of the ugly duckling.

My first chance to shed the image of the ugly duckling came when I was a working adult in my 20s, when my good friend introduced me to the ritual called the 'mirror exercise'. The exercise was to look deeply into my own eyes in a mirror saying affirmations that I am a beautiful soul, full of love and forgiveness. Accepting myself as a beautiful person was very unlike my nature.

The practice made me feel very awkward and uncomfortable, but as I practised with perseverance, it became an enjoyable exercise, and slowly but surely it helped me shed the image of the ugly duckling.

Many years later, a caring friend of mine introduced me to the soul detox program. As the name suggests, it indeed is a soul-cleansing and realigning of images and values, which served my higher purpose. I had my 'aha' moment when my highest calling was revealed in this program. It was truly a life-transforming class in which I learned that my greatest gift is my deep sense of purpose through my writings, especially my poetry. It is truly enlightening to see your own light and greater purpose in life revealed when you anchor yourself through the grounding exercises taught in soul detox. I trust that we all have to detox our souls by letting go of old wounds and negative emotional conditioning in order to transform ourselves into the new celebrities and game-changers that are our true selves.

The Inferiority Complex

The idea that I am inferior because I am not beautiful stemmed from my childhood when I was about seven years old. When my younger sister was born, my parents doted on her and sort of abandoned me. My skin colour was darker than hers because I had inherited my dad's genes, as my mum is the fairer one. My younger sister's skin colour turned out to be a milky white, and when she was born, everyone was cooing at about how beautiful she looked. It was then that the comparisons of skin colour and beauty began between us.

During family engagements and gatherings, I was often humiliated by my own mother. She always joked that after she gave birth to me at the hospital, I was accidentally exchanged for a Black child. As time went on, my sister grew to be a pretty, fair young lady. She was always seen accompanying my mother on visits to my relatives' homes and social gatherings. Just because I was not as fair as my younger sister, my mother avoided bringing me with her on social outings, so from a very young age, I was left alone with my grandparents at home.

Unable to express my anger and yearning for my mother's attention, I grew up with a deep-seated inferiority complex that I am not beautiful, and that only beautiful people get recognized in society. From then on, I had very low self-esteem and thought I couldn't hold a candle to my younger sister's beauty. I always retreated into a corner of my room and cried buckets in silence.

I am very embarrassed to write about my childhood school days, but I have to get this off my chest. In school, I cried over the slightest thing. I was a super-sensitive child whom teachers found hard to deal with. I was socially inept, too, and had very few friends. During recess time, I was always by myself reading in a corner while my classmates had a whale of a time enjoying themselves skipping or playing catch. To be precise, I was a social misfit. My classmates kept their distance from me as I cried rivers over the slightest upsets. I could not handle confrontation or even normal conversation, as I had very few socio-emotional skills.

At home, I never got the approval or attention I felt I deserved. In school, I was labelled a 'crybaby' and shunned by my classmates. I came to the conclusion that there was something wrong with me, as I barely had one good friend.

The Message to Be Seen and Not Heard

We followed a patriarchal regime in my household, and I was not to speak in front of my older brothers. Instead, I sought every one of my family members' attention by speaking up boldly and asserting my opinions and views during dinner and when watching TV as a family. For this, I earned the wrath of my older brothers. My second-oldest brother especially loathed my watching TV with them and condemned and ostracized me. He would chase me away and utter harsh verbal abuses, telling me to, 'Shut up! Leave the living room, and never show your face in here again'!

Time and again, I was humiliated by my older brothers. A tipping point was reached, and I disappeared into my room from then on, totally not bonding with my brothers. I learned that my voice should not be heard by my brothers. To win their approval, I retreated into my own world. I discovered the ultimate escape in books. I was able to vent my frustration by reading about someone else's pain or escape. I became a voracious reader and could see myself in the world of books in which I took the shapes of the beautiful characters in the stories I read.

The Shy Teenager

In my college days, I was a very shy, socially inept, and unconfident young lady. The inferiority complex I felt because I was not beautiful had by now become a part of my psyche. While all my friends in college were going out on dates, I never got a chance to get even one date with any guy. My relationships with men were only platonic and never went beyond friendship. Soon, I believed that men were not attracted to me because I was dark and ugly. I believed that I would only become worthy when a man would take me out and show interest in me.

In order to make up for my self-imposed physical limitation of being dark-skinned, I began to concentrate on my studies, performed reasonably well, completed my major in English with an emphasis in English literature, and went on to complete my Master's in Early Childhood Studies. I also excelled at writing and appreciated poetry.

With the Almighty God's grace and blessings, I became a language teacher. I had a passion for languages and chose to teach the Tamil Language to primary school children. As I connected with young children, I began to heal my old wounds about being an ugly duckling. I became a heroine to the young children who came to me with their little upsets to solve. Soon, I became very energetic in engaging the children under my charge.

However, the message that I am not good enough kept coming back from my teaching colleagues in my teaching profession in one way or another.

My inferiority complex showed up in an inability to bring projects to completion and procrastinating about doing certain aspects of my job. All these were painful reminders of my old conditioning from my childhood. Often, I felt abandoned – like a stringless kite. My inability to bond and interact with my working colleagues in my immediate language department haunted me like my older brothers who had thumped me down, denying me a voice and presence in our home.

My emotional healing and breakthrough came when I attended the self-awareness seminar. As the name suggests, it was indeed a very deep and soul-searching journey to detoxify my soul of old negative conditionings and to better manage the upheavals from all the facets of my life. I learned the art of sincere forgiveness in order to allow abundance and clarity to flow into my life. A great healing took place as I shed tears of release when I began to free myself from my old, negative programming and, most of all, learned to forgive myself. I now shed tears of relief.

I affirmed from that moment on that I am a beautiful and loving soul sent forth by our Creator to this beautiful place called Earth. Now, my soul is set free from being an ugly duckling, and it is a beautiful swan.

I do hope that my life story has enlightened you on your path to healing in one way or another. Always affirm and believe that you are a beautiful soul with a loving and forgiving heart, and let go of feelings of inferiority. You **are** a worthwhile human being.

Power Summary

Let's recap some of the key points in this chapter:

1. What was the self-sabotaging childhood conditioning I received?

2. What was the key lesson I learned in the self-awareness program?

3. What was the impact on my self-esteem as I began to channel my energy on writing poetry and books?

Three Actions You Can Take to Raise Your Self-Esteem

1. **Do Mirror Work Every Day with Positive Affirmations**

Stand in front of a mirror floor-length or even your handphone camera. Look deep into your eyes and embrace the beautiful you staring at yourself and keep saying aloud positive affirmations and releasing statements. Two examples of releasing statements and affirmations are as follows:

a.　I cannot see the light without darkness. Once I remember the difference, I allow the feeling of feeling low to be released. I am happy, whole and healed. So be it, so it is.

b.　I seek connection through the things and experiences that brings me joy. I am re-sparking my connection when my heart feels full.

2.　Taking Time To Love Yourself

This is the way to increase your positive vibrations which, in turn, gives birth to a heightened self-esteem. Loving and taking care of ourselves is not selfish. On the contrary, its self-love. The more care, love, and compassion you show yourself, a more fulfilled and happy, best version of yourself emerges. And with a renewed healthy and happy you, you will be able to offer the best to the people around you. That concept is reflected gracefully in my favourite late Louise Hay's quote:

'Loving myself is my magic wand'.

3.　Journaling Attitude of Gratitude

Every day think of three to five things you are grateful for and write it down in an *Attitude of Gratitude Journal*. Being in a constant state of thankfulness for the things we have increases more of the things we can be thankful for. This is one of the ways to skydive your feel-good hormones and ultimately increase our self-esteem.

"Take action to empower yourself, women! Take action to introduce the transformation that you represent, women! Take action to be the star in your own real-life movie, women! Enough is enough of staying in your own cocoon, women! Enough is enough of suppressing your own dreams, women! Take action to shine your own light to light up other women's light! Take action to welcome the bigger you! Take action to make your dream your signature! Take action to be the new game-changer!"
~ Najmunnisa Abdul Kader~

Love and Blessings,

About the Author

Najmunnisa Abdul Kader is a poet, international best-selling author, Women's Voice Catalyst and Women's Book Coach whose ingenious initiative to step up and bring about change in women entrepreneurs and authors is causing a stir in the world of women. Her ambition is fired by her own awakening, after a roller coaster ride from childhood and finally seeing a light at the end of the tunnel through a three-day soul detox program she underwent in 2015.

She could only master the courage to be creative and grow to take on an avatar of a writer and poet after the soul detox program. From then on, she became unstoppable and went on to co-author a book with internationally acclaimed author and coach, Zai Miztiq, entitled *5 Things That I love About A Women*, which became an international best seller. Then, she went on to author her own book entitled, *Your Dream. Your Signature. A Collection of Soul Touching Poems*.

Najmunnisa feels for the suffering of women who don't take actions in their lives and to step up and be the best version of themselves. She shares this wisdom and empathy through her *Queen* books and poetry.

She has been featured in Singapore's *Vasantham TV Channel*, on the program 'Achamillai Achamillai', a women's talk show. She has also been interviewed for her passion and work by *WurkTV* and the Allahtraunites.Creative Society.

Her greatest happiness stems from seeing her women authors awaken and re-write their own unique stories to become published authors… and awaken women one woman at a time.

Najmunnisa Abdul Kader, Women's Voice Catalyst, is a ghostwriter, an international best-selling author, and a women's book coach who has stepped up to guide and give voice to the women around the world to awaken their best version of themselves. Her coaching and training are causing a ripple among the women, allowing them to reveal their authentic voices and share their unique *Queen* stories on the pages of a book. If you want to turn your pain to power, and need assistance to put it into a book, get in touch with Najmunnisa at any of the following links:

Business Name: Queen N Books

Business Page:
 https://www.facebook.com/WomensVoiceCatalyst/

Email: ishajanu@gmail.com

Facebook: https://www.facebook.com/najmunnisa.kader

LinkedIn: linkedin.com/in/najmunnisa-abdul-kader-78a20a191

I*nstagram*: https://www.instagram.com/womensvoicecatalyst

Poetry Blog: https://www.facebook.com/DiamondToBehold/

Ideal Clients: Women from ages 30-55 years old who are ready to move from pain to power through the art of story-telling.

Books:
https://www.amazon.com/author/najmunnisakader

> *7 Jewels In The Crown: Queen 3*
> https://www.amazon.com/dp/1691823910

> *7 Crowns In The Soul: Queen 2*
> https://www.amazon.com/dp/1983929123

> *Once A Queen Always A Queen: Queen 1*
> https://www.amazon.com/154413777X

> *Your Dream. Your Signature: A Collection of Soul-Touching Poems*
> https://www.amazon.com/dp/1541294351

Fear of Failure. Fear of Success.

N. Green, Sr.
Artist Manager/Music Consultant, Fashion Designer,
Mentor & Coach, U.S.A.

"If you know what losing feels like, it makes it much easier to __win__."
~N. Green. Sr.

The Struggle and Starting from the Bottom

"You think it's easy being me? Well, it ain't never been easy." These are the lyrics from the song "Never Been Easy," a song that I wrote about my life and the heartache, pain, and struggles I have endured.

Where I came from, struggling was just a part of life. I didn't grow up with a silver spoon in my mouth. I was introduced to poverty at a very young age. My mama; my grandma, rest in peace; my great aunt "Bike;" and my aunt "V," rest in heaven; worked together to raise me. Mama worked three jobs when I was very young, and while she was working, grandma took care of my little sister and me. My grandma was a homemaker, but she was also a hustler and knew how to make an extra buck.

Eight of us stayed in a two-bedroom apartment in the urban core, the projects of Kansas City, Missouri. The apartment was in a high-rise, low-income building called Wayne Miner Court, a building that has since been demolished, in an area known to locals as "12th street." For the first 15 years of my life, I only knew this community. Our food came from the neighborhood food pantry, which folks referred to as "welfare rights." Every month, my grandma and I would walk to welfare rights and retrieve our ration. I was a kid who knew how to count books of $5 and $10 food stamps, knew what canned pork and commodity cheese tasted like, and thought that every kid went to the food pantry with their grandma each month. Occasionally, the electricity or the gas was cut off, and we had to warm up a pot of water and take "wash-ups" in the morning before school. There were times when we had to stay over at a relative's house because we were evicted. A couple of times, we were put out of a relative's house and lived out of trash bags because we didn't have a permanent place to stay. You learn very quickly how to be creative and how to improvise.

You see, life wasn't easy for a young Black man in America. There were nights when I felt like I would never amount to anything. There were nights when I needed a shoulder to cry on but felt like I didn't have anyone to turn to for help. It seemed like I was always surrounded by negativity, drama, and violence. If it wasn't for my Almighty Savior and my strong faith, I don't know how things would have turned out for me. I live by the motto "life is what you make it," and that has been my philosophy most of my adult life. It's all about how you make things happen, and these experiences as a young boy shaped me and helped me to become the humble and blessed man that I am today.

Street Smarts and Common Sense

My mama always told me that "closed mouths don't get fed," and my daddy said to "never be a follower, always to be a leader." That advice kept me grounded, disciplined, and focused. I never wanted to be anyone's burden, and I wasn't one to blindly trust someone else's thinking. I carved out my own path, and I was groomed not only by street hustlers and con artists but also by intellectuals and entrepreneurs.

I was raised mainly by women and didn't have a lot of male role models, but the few men that were around had a tremendous impact on my life. When I was four years old, my mama married my stepdad, my sister's daddy. By the time I was six, he had managed to get himself arrested, charged, and convicted of armed robbery. For the next six years, from behind bars, he tried his best to teach me about the good, the bad, and the ugly. He did not want me to follow in his footsteps down a road of destruction.

My grandpa, my mama's daddy, who I called "PawPaw T," was another influential man in my life. PawPaw T was a street pimp and a hustler who moved from Kansas City to Omaha when I was just a baby, and every summer, I spent two weeks with him in Omaha. PawPaw T was originally from Arkansas and was one of ten siblings. He only had a fifth-grade education because in his generation, if you didn't work, you didn't eat. He kept me in line when I stayed with him, and when he thought I was getting too big for my britches, he would let me know. He was honest with me and told me when I was acting spoiled or selfish. I didn't always appreciate that at the time, but looking back, it made me a better person. I cherished the time I spent with PawPaw T. I knew that if he had the opportunity and privileges that I had growing up, he would have been in a better position. PawPaw T inspired me to want more for myself.

Going into seventh grade, I was invited to be a part of a mentoring program that was sponsored by a group of corporate entrepreneurs in the greater Kansas City area. The program, called the "Challenge Program," was geared towards at-risk adolescents who were living in the urban core. Each student was paired up with a mentor with the goal being to successfully build a relationship with the student and make a positive impact in their life.

My mentor was "JB." JB was a young entrepreneur who owned his own business. He was a smooth, well-dressed professional. From the first day we met until my freshman year, I never saw him in anything other than a suit and tie or polo shirt and slacks with dress shoes. He brought me lunch on Thursdays – a steak burrito supreme meal from Taco Bell, and I felt like a King! His philosophy on life was nothing that I had ever experienced, nor heard before. He showed me his world and what life could be for me if I just believed in myself and refused to settle for just being average. He made me want more for myself. He made me think **big!** His drive inspired me to want more in life and to push myself to become more than just a statistic. I wanted what he wanted for me, and I wanted to make him proud.

When I was 14 years old, my mama began dating a guy named "Rizzo." He was everything my mama wanted and needed in a man. He was a hard worker, a great father, and he loved to have fun and make people laugh. Rizzo looked out for me. He got me my first job as a dishwasher at the local Italian bistro where he worked as the kitchen manager, and by age 16, I had worked with Rizzo at three different Italian restaurants. He wasn't just my mama's husband or my stepdad. I considered him my dad. He showed me how to be a man and how to provide for a family. He passed away a few years ago, and I miss him every day. Rest well, Dad.

Musically Motivated and Driven

From a young age, I was drawn to music. And the person that inspired me and put me on that path was my aunt V, my mama's sister. Right after she graduated high school, she packed her bags, got on a Greyhound Bus, and headed for Los Angeles, the city where nobodies become somebodies. When she got there, she moved in with a distant cousin and began her journey into show business. She hired an agent and began doing photoshoots, started going to casting calls, and auditioned for a few small roles in commercials.

I idolized my aunt V, and after an exhilarating visit to California with my grandma at the age of nine, I began writing music. The first song was called "Just A Dream." It was a slow tempo melody about a kiddie crush I had on a girl in my class. As the years went on, my songs got better, and by 13, I was sending demos to my aunt V, who had several friends in the music business. And then finally, when I was 14, I hit big! My aunt V called and told me that one of her industry friends had heard my demo and wanted to offer me a development deal with their label. She suggested that I move to L.A. to pursue this once-in-a-lifetime opportunity. But I was a dumb kid at the time, caught up in a teenage romance, and decided I would wait to move to L.A. until after I graduated from high school. What I didn't realize then was that time waits for no man, so when I did graduate, the opportunity was gone.

Losing out on L.A. didn't stop me from pursuing a career in music. In 1998, I went after it again and became an aspiring rap artist who went by the name Mr. Feddie or Feddie Scrillz. I began recording songs at a local studio called In the Ditch, and started performing at local nightclubs, music venues, and open-mic events. I was religiously sending off material to major record companies in the hopes of getting offered a recording contract.

After a couple of years, I realized that I was wasting my time trying to score a major label record deal, so with the advice of a few veteran musicians, I decided to launch my own independent record label and in 2002, Royalty Mob Records was established. I hit the ground running! By 2004, I had recorded a full-length album, performed in front of hundreds of fans, was featured on a mixtape from a popular DJ from New York City, and had an exclusive interview in a local magazine. I was building rapport and networking with members of the music industry, all the while gaining notoriety in Kansas City and surrounding areas. In 2007, I released the second album from the label and then decided to close the doors to pursue a career outside of music.

I never regretted my decision to stop doing music and I continued to be driven. As part of my new career, I had the opportunity to give back to the community and I wanted to make a difference in other's lives the way JB had made a difference in mine. I became a mentor and a coach for at-risk youth. It was a rewarding and fulfilling job. I met with community leaders, I recruited players for basketball and football teams, I conducted practices, and I helped kids realize that there wasn't just one way to live life.

I like to think that I made a difference, and if I changed the path for at least one kid, I was a success.

Entrepreneurship – It Was All a Dream

My present enterprise, ScrilltownMO, was a vision I had back in 2007, during my days as CEO of Royalty Mob Records. The philosophy for Scrilltown is bigger than just music, bigger than just money, and not just about fashion – it was Scrilltown, Moneytown USA. In December of 2019, I began to develop a plan for creating my holding company, ScrilltownMO, LLC, with subsidiaries ScrilltownMO Management & Consulting and Scrilltown Clothing Company.

ScrilltownMO Management & Consulting would specialize in artist management, artist development, project development, and Artists and Repertoire (A&R) consulting. Scrilltown Clothing Company would be a trendy apparel line. My idea for the company was just the beginning, and I realized that I didn't know everything I needed to know to set up and run a successful business, so I did a lot of research and talked to other successful entrepreneurs. I was persistent and driven, and by the end of January 2020, I had created an LLC, acquired a business license, applied for a tax ID number, and set up my business financials. Next, I worked on establishing the Scrilltown brand.

Establishing your brand is critical, and I knew that, but I also knew that I hadn't been in the music industry for over 13 years. That meant I had to think outside the box and look for new ways to promote myself and my brand because I couldn't promote the way I had back in 2004 – times had changed. I decided to start with my old music, by re-mastering *Runnin'mates*, the album I released under Royalty Mob Records 16 years ago. I re-mastered the album and released it under the ScrilltownMO brand on every digital platform available – *Apple Music*, *Spotify*, *Google*, *Pandora*, *Tidal*, etc. Then I assembled previously unreleased songs that I had recorded over the years and released them under ScrilltownMO as a limited-edition collector's EP.

My strategy worked! I campaigned one single from each of the two albums – "We Rides Dirty" and "I'm Right Here," and before I knew it, the digital streams were rolling in and quickly got up to over 10,000. I wasn't just getting streams, though. I was getting positive feedback from the music community, so I continued to promote my old projects under my new brand. After a time, I decided I needed to start working on new material. I released my first single, a tribute to the woman who taught me the meaning of the phrase "hard work," on Mother's Day 2020 – a song titled "My Mama." The song has been in radio rotation worldwide since it released and has over 100,000 streams on *SoundCloud* and over 10,000 streams on *Spotify*.

Lessons – Music and Fashion Today

I learned a lot starting ScrilltownMO. One thing I learned was that the music promotion game had hugely changed. The days of promoting albums by posting flyers and posters on billboards in nightclubs, music stores (what are those?), or liquor stores were over. When you hand someone a CD, they look at you with a bewildered look on their face. Now, you have to be socially savvy and know what social media tools will promote you best in your industry. And you must be aware that your online presence, who you associate with, and even your personal life, can affect your brand.

Perception is everything when starting up a new business, so manage your entire image carefully. Promote yourself first! Wear your brand in public as much as possible. The more people see your brand, the more they are going to inquire. It only takes one person to change your life. The support of one key person can move you to the next level.

And networking – there isn't enough that can be said about networking. Networking is the key to getting a new business off the ground. You have got to know how to network to get your foot in the door and to continue to move forward. There are a lot of ways you can successfully network. With my clothing line, I first started networking and promoting my product with family and friends. I gave away a lot of ScrilltownMO apparel in the beginning because I knew that if my friends and my family liked my product, they would tell their friends, and word would spread – and it did! Another thing I do as I am networking is to look for win-win business relationships. I have found that people aren't interested in helping you if you aren't willing to help them. An expression we use here at ScrilltownMO is "we support those who support us!" And finally, be aware of the scams. Be vigilant, do your research. If it's too good to be true, it probably is.

The more success you have, the more people will target you and try to destroy everything you've worked hard to secure.

Summary

1.   Promote. Promote. Promote.

2.   Be social savvy and mindful of your online image.

3.   Learn how to effectively network. Networking is the key to success.

4.   Beware of scammers. Someone is always out to steal your shine.

Success Actions

1.   Educate yourself and always be learning. Things change day-to-day. Be ready, be adaptable, and be willing to take on a challenge.

2.   Be driven and hungry for success but be humble at the same time. Never forget where you came from.

3.   Believe in yourself and believe in your brand, and never give up. Your success is entirely up to you.

Throughout my life, I have had ups and downs, dreams and nightmares, failures and success. That's what life is about. No one ever said it was going to be easy. It's up to you to accept the challenge and take hold of your dreams and live your best life.

Nate,

About the Author

N. Green, Sr. is a former indie label CEO, now an Artist Manager, Fashion Designer, and Mentor & Life Coach for at-risk youth. He started writing music at the age of nine years old. By age 14, he was offered a development recording contract with a major record label. In 2002, he launched his own independent record label, Royalty Mob Records. From 2002 to 2007, he owned and operated the label and managed several hip-hop artists in the Kansas City area. In 2007, he decided to pursue a career outside of music and was allowed to give back to his community by organizing programs for at-risk teens, mentoring them, and preparing them for life after graduation. In 2020, with a vision that he had during his music days, he launched ScrilltownMO, a management and consulting company. ScrilltownMO specializes in Artist Management, Artist Development, Project Management, and A&R Consulting. Scrilltown Clothing, a subsidiary, is the visual embodiment of the company's slogan "Money, Music, & Fashion."

In his spare time, he likes to travel. He has dreams of one day of establishing a not-for-profit organization that will provide young individuals with the skills they need to survive in the real world.

Contacts

Business Name: ScrilltownMO LLC

Website: https://scrilltownmobusiness.com/

Online Clothing Store: https://shop.spreadshirt.com/scrilltown-clothing-company/

Facebook Management Company:
https://www.facebook.com/pg/Scrilltownmo-Management-Consulting-104168444528229/

Facebook Clothing Company:
https://www.facebook.com/Scrilltown-Clothing-Company-102920381404758/

LinkedIn: https://www.linkedin.com/in/scrilltownmo/

About ScrilltownMO Management & Consulting

Are you looking for management, consulting, and /or representation that you can trust, or maybe for just some advice on your next project/album?

At ScrilltownMO, the services that we provide can come in a variety of ways: We provide digital platform playlist promos (*Spotify, SoundCloud*, etc.). We also offer social media promoting (*Facebook, IG*, etc., and music blogs), radio interview scheduling, and we also can submit your music for possible Internet or international radio spins or song placements/licensing.

Ideal Clients:

Unsigned Artist	Comedians
DJ's/Radio	Record Labels
Beatmakers	Comedians

About Scrilltown Clothing Company

Our mission is to lead by example. We represent Music, Money, & Fashion. We don't judge, as long as you get money "by any means necessary."

Ideal Clients:

Models	Fashion Designers

You Can Overcome Anything Despite the Barriers in Life

Nor Suhir
Certified Social Media Strategists and Business Coach, Singapore

*There is **only one me**. It's my **own** journey. What makes me **different**? I **decide** the ending.*
~ Nor Suhir

The Meltdown

December 2015 is a month I will never forget. I suffered my first stroke. Two weeks later, I suffered a second stroke which caused my retina to detach. After that incident, from one eye, I saw complete darkness, while the other was just a blur. A few months later, I suffered yet another stroke. This was the start of a four-year journey that changed my life forever. I became an infant again. I had to learn how to talk because my speech was slurred. I had to learn how to eat – how to chew and swallow – so that whatever I consumed did not end up choking me instead. I had to learn how to climb stairs, how to hold a pen, pick up coins, and other small items. The list goes on and on.

Doctors were unable to immediately reattach my retina because of the stroke, so I had to learn to do all those things with almost zero vision. When they finally managed to operate on my eye, life decided it was not done with me. That same retina detached again after a few weeks. I had to go through a series of eye surgeries just to get my vision back.

The physical therapy from the stroke was exhausting. I wanted to throw in the towel several times. I used to be a cheerful and outgoing person who was always active. As a consultant and coach, my days were filled with meetings and appointments with clients. Networking, training and coaching sessions filled my daily schedule. Engaging with an audience on stage felt like second nature, but with the blink of an eye, I had to be confined to a bed. I did not have the strength to move around on my own, even if I used a walking stick. Someone had to accompany me everywhere I went. I lost count of the number of times I visited the hospital in those four years. It became a second home.

It did not take long before I became sad and depressed. I felt ashamed to appear in public. I became reserved and timid but did what I could to keep my feelings to myself and not show it to my family because I knew they were feeling stressed-out too. My son had to sacrifice his studies by taking two semesters off to take care of me. It made him lose his scholarship.

I have always been the backbone of the company. The multiple strokes caused my business to go into pause mode. We were unable to bring in new clients because of my inability to move around. One-by-one, members of my team had to leave because we did not have enough money to pay them. We had to be prudent since there was barely any income. I was not afraid of shutting the company down if I had to because I believed that when my health got better, I could build it back up. But, what did make me fearful was the possibility that my health would not improve, that I would lose my eyesight forever and not be able to speak normally since the stroke attacks affected the parts of the brain that controlled speech. If I was unable to see and speak, how could I rebuild my business?

Fortunately, I was soon able to move around with the help and support of my family. At that point, I knew I had to muster the courage to meet people. I cannot run a business hiding at home, life must go on.

Having to put up a happy front to clients was a challenge. Pretending I could see them even when all I saw were only shades of grey was nerve-wracking. I gave the excuse that I was having a bad, sore throat during business meetings when people could not understand me. I was afraid that they would find out that my speech was slurred and that I had forgotten what I had wanted to say in the middle of a conversation. What would happen if my clients found out about my health issues? Would they terminate the contract? Would they still trust me to finish the job? I believed that, deep down, I was still the same person with the same capabilities, especially when it came to business strategy and helping my clients get new customers. It was only my physical state that was affected, but would they continue to believe in me? We needed the money. There was a lot of uncertainty, anxiety and stress, and it was crippling.

I had to start believing that I could do the job again!

There were so many negative thoughts. I experienced anxiety attacks and extreme stress. I could not explain how I felt. I wanted to break down and cry after every meeting because I was not able to convey what I had in mind effectively. It felt as if my mind was working faster than my ability to speak.

One day, my husband and son had a heart-to-heart talk with me. They advised me to stop focusing on the handicap. They reassured me that I am good at what I do, despite the disabilities. I had to draw my focus back on why I started the business and what makes me happy – my passion for helping others grow their business.

Worrying about the things that I have no control over will not make me happy. It will not help me, my family, or my clients. At that point, I sat down and reflected on everything that had happened. I had to make a decision – either I sink with self-pity or swim to the shore and pick myself back up.

The Turning Point

It took me a good three years to pick myself back up. I was able to walk on my own without a walking stick. I was able to talk without slurring, even though I had to speak slower. I was able to visit the hospital on my own. Even though my vision remained greyish, I was able to see the outline of a body, so I knew I would not bump into anyone anymore.

On September 2019, I finally got my full vision back. I cannot explain how happy and relieved I was when I saw the blue sky, the greenery, read a car plate, read the signboards, and saw people's faces. It took a good ten minutes for everything to sink in. That feeling remains indescribable. Then, on 11 September, my birthday, I made a vow to rebuild my business. I vowed to grow it bigger than ever. I made a resolution to focus on automation so that my business and my clients' businesses will continue not only to survive but also to thrive in any situation or economy.

I spread out my business risk by diversifying my investments in other companies. I started putting my skills, knowledge, and training materials onto online platforms. I shared my health issues with my mentor, Ms Tina Williams from Bold Angels. She understood what I went through because she was also a stroke survivor. But most importantly, she was a friend when I needed one the most and was someone with whom I could resonate. With Tina's help, I started to rebuild my business. She guided me on how to handle my current situation and urged me to go back to the basics of what she taught me when I first became a Certified Social Media Strategist.

I went back to the drawing board with my husband and son and began strategizing my business goals. I mustered the courage to go out and talk to potential clients face-to-face. Yes, I stuttered. Yes, I stumbled. Yes, I had to pause frequently throughout the meetings and presentations. Even though I felt like I had failed and fell flat on my face after each meeting and presentation, I kept persevering. I kept falling, but I also kept getting back up. I have always believed that how one gets up is crucial. I was relentless in the effort I put into my work. I kept telling myself repeatedly, *I must do it for my family. I am great. I am a fighter. I attract business everywhere I go.*

The Impact

We received an email from a potential client that I did a presentation to a year prior. She saw the transformation that I achieved for a neighbouring business when I was their coach. I was able to achieve in less than a year what she had been trying to do for two years. The client gave us the job, and it boosted my confidence by 1,000,000%!

I started working diligently with the client, strategizing and transforming the business through automation and implementing internal systems. I helped introduce new products and services that were scalable and have now part of their core offerings and have grown to become their main revenue stream. The best part – it was all achieved in less than two years.

At the same time, I also started working on transforming my own business and bringing it into the online space. I created new online training courses to help businesses digitize. I mustered the courage to record videos, conduct *Facebook LIVE* sessions and dug deep into building systems that help to completely automate businesses' sales funnels. The 2020 pandemic situation motivated me to help more businesses acquire new customers through automation. I found mentors that could help guide me in crafting my 'Unlocking Multiple 6-Figure Business Formula'. I worked on my system, started building automation software, and taught the psychological secrets to being a leader with a vision and mission. I focused on helping others believe in their identity and use it to find new opportunities. Pouring all of my efforts into helping others gave me a new perspective on my own business.

A year later, I mustered the courage to apply everything that I had learned in a two-month-long campaign with a client. It was the only client I had at that point. It was either sink or swim. After two months, the business generated almost 700 new customers and $70,000 in additional sales. But, I knew one success was not enough. I approached another potential client and took a big risk – I told them that they did not have to pay me unless I was successful because I wanted to do a proof-of-concept. It was an industry that has a lot of restrictions due to the nature of the business. I needed to not only prove to the client that my system worked, but also prove to myself that I could do it. To cut the story short, I helped the business generate close to 140 new customers within a two-month period. It boosted my self-confidence, and I knew I found my jackpot.

But that was still not enough. I spent more time working on a system that was duplicable and scalable. A system that could be implemented with minimal effort, irrespective of the level of skill of the person implementing it.

Today, as I am writing this, I am happy to share that my system is currently being implemented by my clients.

The Belief Will Set You to Help Others Too

I help business owners acquire the skills and develop the systems needed to unlock their multiple six-figure business and thrive in any economy. I am a 'Rainmaker' in the small business world with the abilities to identify ideal customers for any business. For those who share the same dream but have yet to realize it, I believe I can help them finally become a 'Rainmaker'. Not only will they have the ability to build a multiple six-figure business but they will also be empowered to help others too.

In August 2020, I launched my own automation platform, *ChatEngaged*, which has helped automate 90% of the work that I do with my clients. The interesting part about using my platform and system is that it has helped my clients be 'Rainmakers' themselves. It was no longer just about me, it was also about them helping themselves and others.

Key Lessons and Words of Wisdom

Giving up is not an option. My new journey of transformation has only just begun. It is as if I have been reborn. The chapters of my life prior to my stroke has long ended. My focus should be in the present and in the possibilities that the future holds. The tide will turn at the right place and time.

You will never know what you might find when you take the first step. Trust yourself. You are a leader with a vision and mission to help others. You just need to train your mind to default towards success.

There will never be a proverbial, perfect time to start. You need to just take that first step. You will fall, but what matters is that you get up again. You will make mistakes, but you will overcome them. It was because I took my first step that I was able to achieve the things that I thought was impossible before. The wheels are now in motion, and it is not going to stop any time soon.

Within one year of my full recovery, I was able to launch my own customer-generating system and positioned myself as an authority, expert, and influencer in my field. Now, I help entrepreneurs build a 'Rainmaker' for their business and others through my free masterclass:

http://norsuhir.com/weeklymasterclass

All these would not have been possible if I had not taken that first step.

After going through the process, I have listed the key lessons learned in my path to success, below. Give yourself permission to be you. Control your identity because it is 100%-based on your action.

Wisdom #1 – Believe in Yourself

Through this journey, from the day I suffered my first stroke until now, I came to realize that my self-belief was what led me to turn my life around. It has helped me change my life and my environment. I am me. I am unique. I create my own reality by asking who I am going to be, who I want to be in my future reality, and build an emotional connection with myself and my goals.

Wisdom #2 – Be a Leader

This is **me**. I need to focus on my direction, brand, and impact on my audience. Build a proven framework that is clear, scalable, and generates predictable recurring cash flow that is easily duplicable. As a leader, I must help others be successful as it is never just about me alone.

Identify my 'why' and what I can do to step things up, and influence and impact my audience positively. There are many out there who teach what I teach. But I know that there is **only one me**, and that makes me special. I use this to position myself and focus on filling the gaps in my target audiences' needs.

Wisdom #3 – Strong Backend System

Systems are an important piece that's missing in most businesses. It is a formula that guides your actions and business decisions in order for you to achieve your goals and objectives.

One of my business' backend systems is my ACC formula – Attract, Connect, Convert. The main purpose of the ACC formula is having conversations with my audience that will eventually convert. My objective when applying it is to generate one appointment a day consistently.

Every business needs a strong backend system. People out there focus too much on putting out content. Content alone will not bring me paying customers if I have a weak or non-existent system that ties all my marketing activities into a cohesive flow. When I develop and implement my backend system, my business changes tremendously.

Your backend system can help you build relationships with your audience.

Wisdom #4 – Take Action

For a journey to begin, you need to take the first step. However, how far you are willing to go is determined by your motivation to succeed. It all starts with your attitude, a clear vision and that courageous first step. If I can do it, there is no reason why you cannot.

The Rewards

I am grateful that now I am able to move around independently and talk to people, especially strangers, without stuttering. I am grateful that I am able to help my clients build their businesses. I am grateful that my business that had to stall due to my poor health is now slowly but surely coming back up again.

My journey has only just begun, and I have no intention of stopping any time soon. I am extending my hand to you to share your story and to come and walk our respective journeys together. I know some of you have to swim hard to keep your heads above the water, but I want to be there for you. You never know, your rainbow might just be around the corner.

Recently, I was invited to be the President of the Hawkerentrepreneur Chapter at International Business Federation Singapore in order to help local F&B businesses digitalize. I also finally launched my own backend system *Messenger* bot, *Chatengaged*. Now, I teach business owners all around the world to be 'Rainmakers' and unlock their multiple six-figure and thrive in any economy. Be a 'Feedompreneur'!

http://norsuhir.com/weeklymasterclass

You are a 'Freedompreneur' when you have people chasing to buy from you because you have a proven framework that delivers insane results. You have built a brand that impacts others because your Magnetic Message resonates with others.

Power Summary

Giving up is not an option.

My unique message is what connects me with my audience. It gives me the ability to help others.

For my business to attain a multiple six-figure income and have a constant stream of new leads, I need to set up a strong backend system.

Success Actions

1. Your online business relies on three key aspects – Traffic, your Sales Conversion Process, and your High-Perceived Value Offer.

2. Focus on selling the outcome. People buy based on emotions and use logic to justify their actions.

3. Set up your duplicable and scalable backend system that aligns your audience into your acquisition system. The main focus of this backend system is to help your audience solve their most immediate problem.

"I do not live to make my presence noticed. I am unique. My story is unique. My journey is unique. I want my absence to be felt because I live for a cause!"
~ Nor Suhir

With Love and Blessings. Be Healthy

Nor Suhir

About the Author

Nor Suhir is a stroke survivor, Certified Social Media Strategist, Business Coach, and author of the upcoming book, *You Can Overcome Anything Despite the Barriers in Life.* She is also the President of the Hawkerentrepreneur Chapter at International Business Federation, Singapore, helping local food and beverage businesses digitalize, and recently launched her own *Messenger* automation application, *ChatEngaged.*

Contacts

You Can Overcome Anything Despite the Barriers in Life:

http://norsuhir.com

ChatEngaged: http://chatengaged.com

Confidence and Courage

Nour Tarzi
CEO, Tarzi Design Studio, USA

"Take a leap of faith and follow your intuition because all that you need to fly is confidence & courage."
~ Nour Tarzi

The Meltdown

It was 2004 and I was standing in the LAX International Airport waiting for my sister to arrive from Syria. Being at the airport brought back memories from two years earlier when I had come to the USA for the first time with my mom and sister.

I came from Syria, full of dreams and hopes. My goal was to study at a good university. Living in California was my chance to learn what I liked: computer art, graphic design, and animation. Little did I know that it was not that easy to get into a school, especially since I didn't speak English and couldn't afford the tuition!

A friend advised me to visit Long Beach City College and start my education there. However, since I had just recently moved only recently to California, the school considered me an international student, which meant the tuition would be costly. To be considered a California resident, I needed to have lived in California for a year. Every single day during that year, I drove by the school on Carson Blvd., watching the students crossing the street from the parking structure to the campus. God knows how much I wished to cross that street with them. That day finally came.

It had been a year since I had my driver's license. Finally, I could register at the community college as a resident. However, I tried to register, only to find out that the deadline for registration had passed. I had to wait for another four months to pass until the next semester! During that year, my mom and my sister struggled with the culture shock, so they decided to go back to Syria. It was up to me to either go back with them or stay in the USA to pursue my dream of studying. I still remember the warm tears on my cheeks and remember the prayers I made to God to help me make the right decision. I decided to stay alone in California and be apart from my family for the first time in my life.

Back then, the Internet was new. Smartphones and messenger apps did not exist, and there was no way to talk to my family over the Internet. International phone calls were expensive, just like everything else in California.

Having a job is excellent; looking for a job is not! When I mentioned that I was looking for a job to my friends and family around me, they attacked me with all sorts of cruel remarks like, "You don't speak the language!", "You dress differently!", and "Your style is old!" One lady even told me that I look like a mommy. I used to hide in the restroom and cry. God only knows how much I cried, but I was lucky to have a friend in a different state. He encouraged me to go out with my grandmother wherever she goes, even if it was just to the market, and apply for jobs everywhere, and that I did. I asked every single store for a job until a rug store hired me as a cashier.

For two years, I lived with my grandmother. I didn't get out of the house very much except for a few hours because I worked parttime at Lakewood Mall. I used to leave home at 8 a.m. I would arrive at the mall and get a cup of coffee and cookies. No one was there for me to drink coffee with, but the cookies were the only daily joy I had! During lunch breaks, I used to go to McDonald's and sit alone and eat a large meal with Coca-Cola. Before I realized it, I was becoming very overweight, depressed, and a sad little girl!

I was still waiting at the airport for my sister, lost in my thoughts. I was so excited to see her again. My mom wasn't able to get her passport due to issues with her job in Syria. At least I would have my sister who would be visiting for a few weeks. I would have someone to accompany me. I spent a month dreaming of spending the time with her how I would take her to Starbucks so I didn't end up drinking my coffee alone.

"Nour, the airplane landed. Let's get closer to the gate. Your sister will come out soon," my grandmother's voice brought me back to the present, and we walked toward the gate.

Travelers started to come out one after the other, and my eyes were fixed on the gate, waiting for my sister – only to see her with my mom!

My mom wanted to surprise me, so she hadn't told me that she was able to come.

I don't remember what happened at that moment. I wasn't able to see it anymore. I lost control in the airport and yelled very loudly. Everyone's attention turned towards me. I then fell to the floor, crying. I don't remember how long I stayed on the floor crying; I only remember my mom's voice telling me, "It's okay. I am here now!"

The Turning Point

There are a lot of points where you pick yourself up and choose to continue. Success is not a straight line going upwards; it's about failing forward.

I was doing so well at my job that the owner promoted me to be the store manager. The business owner was incredibly supportive during my first few years in California. I learned *QuickBooks* so that I could manage the inventory and accounting for the store. I changed the store interior design and chose the merchandise. Again, when you do your part, the right people show up in your life to help you get there. After two years, he offered me to be a fifty-percent partnership in the business!

Yes, I walked in as a cashier and walked out as a fifty-percent partner!

After graduating from college, I met my prince charming! Things happened very quickly. We were married in less than six months. Ahmad was the best thing that ever happened to me. Not long afterward, I got pregnant with my princess, Sham.

My daughter was only a few months old while I was working as a website designer for a small company that barely paid anything. One night, my girl had a high temperature, and we had to rush her to the emergency room. We came back home early the following morning, and we were all exhausted. I slept for only one hour and then had to go to work! I knew my daughter needed me so badly, but I had no choice but to go to work. An hour later, I received a phone call from my sister, who was watching my daughter, letting me know that my daughter needed me. I walked into the CEO's office – he was a bully – and told him, "I have to take the day off, and if you want to fire me, go ahead!"

That day was the most significant turning point in my life. I knew then that I had to start my own business to be there for my daughter when she needed me, and no one could ever fire me again!

The Impact

It was 2009. I built a simple website, and I offered one service: website design. A friend printed a business card with my name and phone number and told me to join a networking group. I looked up a local networking group and found one in Lakewood. The cost was $450 a year, which was a big investment for me. At that time, I was still working as an employee at a small company, but I changed my work schedule to free up one day to build my business and promote myself. I decided to pay the $450 on a credit card and join the networking group. It was a significant risk for me, but I was looking for a change, and I knew I had to trust myself and my ability to bring in sales. I submitted my application to join the group, and a few days later, I got a phone call asking me to come for an interview. The lady who interviewed me was an interior designer. I offered to redesign her website for $800, and I got the job and my return on investment from the interview!

Working in the evenings on projects and going to work during the day was my life for over a year. With my daughter on my lap, I built many websites for local businesses. My clients educated me on the business aspects of things, such as writing a proposal and issuing an invoice.

I proceeded to build my business with only courage,

The Truth Will Set You Free

I expanded my networking activities, met new CEOs, and got introduced to more companies. I grew my business to have ten in-office employees in the Anaheim office. The pressure became too much growing my business, so I changed the business model to be virtual. Now, all of my employees and contractors are online-based, and I got myself a fancy virtual office. Today I run my business from anywhere globally. All I need is a computer and the Internet! I enjoy life with my kids while still having the revenue coming in.

I am not trying to make it sound easy because it isn't! but it's possible. I started my business, Tarzi Design Studio, when my daughter was only a few months old, and now we are celebrating ten years in business. During those ten years, I have helped hundreds of small and Fortune 500 companies with all of their visual communication design needs. I 've done projects for 3M, Fujitsu, and many more.

I also went back to school and finished my bachelor's degree in visual art. I improved my English skills and became a public speaker sharing my ideas with the world.

Key Lessons and Words of Wisdom

Through adversity, I found strength, learned how to solve problems, and most importantly, I learned how to be happy. By nature, humans seek to be loved, accepted, and as a result, successful and happy. Everyone deserves to be satisfied, and it's not hard. Happiness is a state of mind and understanding that you can gain inner peace regardless of adversity.

Knowing what I now know, I list below the vital lessons which have contributed to transforming my life and business.

Wisdom #1: Adaptability

Society, business, and culture are changing constantly and quickly, and you should change as well. The longer it takes for you to adapt to change, the more internal suffering you will have.

The faster you adapt, the happier and more successful you will be.

Wisdom #2: Relationship

You have perhaps heard that money is power, but, based on my experience, I can tell you that relationships are the real source of strength in your personal and business life.

When you nurture personal relationships, you will find people that will support you during difficult times. Building a business relationship is my number one success in business. When your business colleague knows your mission and believes in you, you will be able to close more deals and win more clients. Moreover, suppose you are interested in charity and helping people in need. In that case, relationships will allow you to go the extra mile, and you don't personally need to have the money, but through your network, you will be able to raise funds for your project.

Wisdom #3: Keep Improving

The greatest asset you have is you, so invest time and money on your growth. As Dr. Stephen R. Covey said, *"We must never become too busy sawing to take time to sharpen the saw."* Your personal and business growth is essential to your success, so never stop improving.

Wisdom #4: Healthy Lifestyle

Steve Jobs said, *"Eat your food as your medicine. Otherwise, you have to eat medicine like your food."* If your health is poor, you have nothing! Your body is the machine that you use 24/7 and is the same machine that will drive you to succeed and attain happiness. No matter what stage of life you are in, no matter how you feel and whether you like to work out or not, or whether you want to eat healthily or not, do it anyway.

Wisdom #5: Confidence, Courage, and Self-image

If there is one secret to my success, it would be confidence and courage!

You are enough the way you are! Don't compare yourself to anyone. Compare yourself only to yourself and try to be better than you were yesterday. Step outside your comfort zone – you might be scared, you might have a chill in your body, you might freeze, and your heart might beat quickly. Learn how to manage your fears and do it anyway. I was the only woman in a conference room of men in L.A.; I did it anyway. I was the sole business owner in my family, and I did it anyway.

Wisdom #6: Practice Empathy

Empathy is one of the essential skills you need in life, but what is empathy? According to The Greater Good Science Center at the University of California, Berkeley, *"Empathy is the ability to sense other people's emotions, coupled with the ability to imagine what someone else might be thinking or feeling."* If you learn how to practice empathy, you will be a better team leader. You will know how to negotiate and create a win-win situation. You will do better at job interviews, sales, and customer service because understanding people helps you win. Show people kindness and mercy. You never know what they have been through.

Wisdom #7: Live to give

"Focus on being a blessing."
~ from *Your Best Life Now* by Joel Osteen.

You probably have heard this advice from almost every successful entrepreneur, but you need to listen to it one more time. As long as you are focused on money and yourself and what you need, you will never feel fulfilled.

A great life includes something worth living for – something bigger than yourself, something that inspires you, pushes you forward, something that only you can offer with your touch that makes a difference in the world around you. Knowing that you are helping people is empowering and makes you feel fulfilled and, as a result, happy.

Wisdom #8: Build a Brand Platform for Yourself and Your Business

What is Branding?

Intelligent, smart, and significant people are talking about branding! Companies, non-profit organizations, countries, and even regions are branded.

So, what is branding?

We all heard that branding is not a logo; it's not a design. But then what is it?

According to Norwich Business School, branding is confidence, passion, belonging, action, security – a set of unique values.

The founder of Amazon, Jeff Bezos, said, *"Branding is what people say about you when you are not in the room."*

"A brand is a name, term, sign, symbol, design, or a combination of them intended to identify goods and services of one seller or group of sellers and differentiate them from those of their competitors."
~ AMA (American Marketing Association) definition

Who needs branding?

Everyone! No matter what you do in life, or what product you sell, everyone and every product or service have a brand. Whether you know it or not, you personally already have a brand. Every product or service already has a brand, even if it was unintentional.

Leaders need to brand themselves also. We follow leaders who we believe in, so if you want to be a leader, you must give us something to believe in. You need to make us see you as a leader by communicating leadership skills and higher values to us. Regardless of whether you are leading a country, company, or family, you need to position yourself as a leader in your audience's eyes.

Build a platform.

To grow your business and make more money, you need to build a system. A platform allows you to expand your reach and do more with less time. If you try to grow your business without a system in place, you're wasting time and energy. Utilize software to your advantage, such as a customer relationship management system, digital marketing platforms, and automated marketing.

The Reward

Today I look back at my life and realize how blessed and thankful I am as my business is scaling, and at the same time, I get to work from anywhere in the world.

When the COVID-19 pandemic hit and the kids had to stay at home, I got to stay at home with them while serving my clients. When I took my kids to visit their grandmother in Syria for six weeks, I was able to run my business from overseas. On the way back to the US, we went to Istanbul, Turkey, for ten days to enjoy the beautiful culture, sights, and food. Since my husband's unachieved dream is to be a pilot, I could get him a training session in which he got to fly over Los Angeles.

I was nominated to be the president of my Toastmasters club. I lead the club to the highest designation "President Distinguished" for the first time in many years; the club has been President Distinguished since then. I also was nominated and served as an area director in Toastmasters and vice president of marketing for The National Association of Women Business Owners, Orange County chapter.

I helped hundreds of small and Fortune 500 companies build their brand online.

When you believe in yourself and embrace change, your life will start to transform.

If I was able to weather the story and challenges on the way to where I am now starting with practically nothing, can you imagine what you can accomplish on your own?

Power Summary

Let me recap some of the key points in this chapter:

- The founder of Amazon, Jeff Bezons said "Branding is what people ___________________."
- Who needs branding?
- Take a leap of faith and follow your intuition because all what you need to fly is _________ and __________.

Success Actions

Here are three success actions that you can do to help you be successful:

1.   Read *The Seven Habit of Highly Effective People.*

2.   Improve your website to reflect who you are, and if you don't have a website, please invest in a professional website and professionally taken photos. Make sure your business website is up to date and reflects the user experience that your brand provides.

3.   Wake up every day with a mission to be happy today.

"Embrace change!"

Love and blessings,

Nour Tarzi

About the Author

Nour Tarzi, designer at heart, is the founder and CEO of Tarzi Design Studio, who is focused on Branding, Marketing, and implementing Web Technologies for local and global, small to mid-sized businesses using major content management systems, customer relation management, Inventory management software and much more.

Being engaged in the field of online marketing since high school, Nour has been an effective marketing professional, who generated an ongoing source of income for her clients.

Experience and talent are not her two sole qualifications in the digital world. Nour majored in computer art, as well as, earning a degree in fine arts. Seeking to broaden her professional expertise and gain a higher level of understanding in her domain of work, she has received certificates involving 3D design, animation, and web design. Moreover she earned a certificate in branding from UCLA extension and Nour is a google analytics and Adwords qualified individual.

She has also enriched her passion and appreciation for art by volunteering at the Long Beach Museum of Art, and Nicholas & Lee Begovich Gallery.

During her free time, Nour enjoys oil painting, reading, and creating crafts with her kids.

Contacts

Website: www.TarziDesignStudio.com
www.NourTarzi.com

Email: nour@tarzidesignstudio.com

Facebook: www.facebook.com/TarziDesignStudio

LinkedIn: www.linkedin.com/in/nourtarzi

Find Your Voice

Razia Naqvi-Jukes
Personal Brand Photographer, UK

'It's not what you are that holds you back, it's what you think you are not.'
~ Razia Naqvi-Jukes

The Meltdown

Imposter syndrome was one of the biggest struggles I have faced all my life.

So, when I changed my career from being a teacher to a photographer, the perceptual thoughts that have sat with me all my life came flooding back. *I'm not a real photographer. I'm a teacher. My degree is in teaching, not photography. I'm not creative enough.* My internal thoughts would circle in my mind continuously, and they would follow me on every shoot in the early days.

Thinking back, I feel I've always struggled with being an imposter. I remember being in class in primary school, and the teacher using me as an example of being a model student. I wasn't smart, not in the traditional way. School was a struggle. But somehow, I was getting away with being in the top sets. I found it so hard to keep up with the teacher and focus for the whole lesson. As long as I could make it look like I was listening and quietly doing my work, I could pull off being a model student. It was the mid-80s, and teachers didn't have the same accountability as they have now. Somehow, I got away with it until a simple class test revealed that I belonged to the bottom sets. The shame was deep and cutting. It was soul-destroying. I remember the shock on my classmates' faces when they realised I didn't belong in the top sets. Dyslexia didn't have a voice then. You were either stupid or intelligent. There were no other labels. Despite my external smiles, deep down, I felt unworthy and not good enough.

I took these feelings of unworthiness with me into my adult life. They echoed in everything I did. Lack of self-worth is so crippling. It influences every decision you make. In my case, it affected the decisions I made when choosing the subjects I studied. I didn't select the subjects I loved; I chose subjects I thought I could do easily. I decided to be a primary school teacher instead of a secondary school teacher because primary school has got to be easier, right? (No offence intended to primary school teachers.) I soon learnt primary school teaching wasn't the more comfortable option. There is a big difference between loving something and choosing safer options. I always played it safe.

The Turning Point

But playing it safe stopped being an option when my husband left me. In 2007, I was a single mum with three very young children. I was depressed, shocked, and overwhelmed for the first six months of his leaving. I was unable to do anything other than the simplest, most basic tasks. I'd manage to get the children to school and then sleep until school pick up time. I lacked energy and the enthusiasm to do anything. I knew I had to find a way out of the terrible spiral of pain that crippled me. I had to be a better mother for the sake of my children.

Something made me pick up the camera and start photographing my children. I started documenting their everyday life. It was beautiful watching and observing them – the way they played, the way they interacted with one another. I observed the light. I developed ways of anticipating the moment, and mostly I noticed something magical unfolding.

I started to notice the beauty in the everyday. Observing life through the lens helped me focus on the beauty that existed already in my life. The feelings of hurt and unworthiness started to change to feelings of gratitude. The truth is, the beauty in my life was always there. I just had to stop and see it. I remember reading a quote at the time that resonated with me.

'It's not what you look at that matters, it's what you see.'
~ Henry David Thoreau

I was seeing for the first time through the lens of gratitude.

I Found My Voice

Alongside this, my photography just got better and better. My kids were young toddlers, and they never stayed in one place for long. Acting fast and knowing I didn't have enough time to get the shot meant I had to move quickly. I was flourishing, growing, and for the first time in my life, I had a voice. Photography gave me a voice. It allowed me to put all my feelings of hurt into my work and turn that pain into something beautiful. It allowed me to express myself in a way I couldn't before. It was almost like speaking without words. My images encapsulated everything I felt, and that felt liberating. I was free. Free because I was heard. Free because I could express myself. Free because I was redefining my newly found self-worth from purely being able to express myself.

I shone, and I could feel it! There was a newfound confidence in me that all could see.

Other mums soon picked up the uniqueness in my work, and after an exhibition of my work, I was asked to photograph a wedding.

The feelings of unworthiness started to make their way to the surface. *I'm going to mess up. I only have one chance to get it right. People are going to know I'm not a real photographer. Photographing a wedding is going to expose the holes in my work. What if the light is too low? What if I mess up the key shots? I won't get the chance to do them again.*

The Breakthrough

I remember when I got my first wedding booking. I spent two weeks running through the wedding timeline in my head and thinking of all the different scenarios that could happen on the wedding day. I rehearsed where I would stand for each shot, and I envisioned how each image would look. The run-up to the wedding was so scary. The fear of being an imposter reared its ugly head again.

But, I knew I had to do it and breakthrough. Pulling out wasn't an option. I just had to stop focusing on my fear and start focusing on what I wanted to accomplish. I had to focus on what the end result would look like. I wanted to achieve beautiful, storytelling images that my lovely bride and groom would look upon and relive. I wanted to create the same beauty that healed me, but for others to enjoy. What I wanted was to give my couple a legacy that they could leave to their children and their children's children, a glimpse of whom they once were. I wanted to capture each couple uniquely and authentically. I found myself doing it again. I was given a voice, but this time my vision and lens became a voice to tell other people's stories.

So, with all the fear of failure in my heart, I left early to shoot the wedding. From the first click of my shutter, something amazing happened. My anxiety disappeared, and I fell into a surreal zone where everything slowed down. I was able to see images before they happened, just as I had visualised. I was using my feelings of empathy to synch in with the emotions surrounding me to anticipate other people's reactions. By doing so, I was able to foresee the moment and be at the right place at the right time.

That night, I loaded my images to the computer with much anticipation. *Did I get the shots I needed?* Well, the pictures I got were amazing! I was so proud of them, and I had proven to myself that I could achieve for others what I did for myself.

Unexpected Results

My '**why**' was now bigger than my fear. The very thing that lifted me was now my purpose for others. Had I stopped with my fear, I wouldn't have achieved the breakthrough for my brand, and the best was yet to come!

I refined my style and my brand. My brand stood for images with emotion, beautiful light, and connection. I got better and better with each wedding. And then, I was noticed by a *YouTuber* and lifestyle influencer Lily Pebbles. She loved my work. I remember Lily saying how she went through so many photographers' portfolios and loved the softness and emotion in my work. It spoke to her. I was so nervous about this wedding as it was a high-profile wedding. *Had I bitten off more than I could chew? Was I going to get found out?* If I don't do a good job, it could ruin my career. The same fears crept back into my mind, but I had to remind myself to focus on the outcome I wanted and not my fear. If I focus on the fear, it will stop me from moving forward. By focusing on the outcome and visualising it, it would become my reality. This magic equation has never let me down.

Her wedding was a success! Lily texted me straight away after seeing her gallery of pictures. She told me she was 'blown away by them'! I went on to photograph the wedding of another influencer, Samantha Maria. Sam booked me after seeing Lily Pebbles' pictures. Their pictures were published in magazines. They were getting anywhere from 60,000 to 100,000 Likes on *Instagram* every time they were used. I noticed that in every subsequent wedding I photographed after these two, I was seen as a celebrity by the brides I photographed. My brand had moved to the next level.

Understanding the power of my brand and how it helped me stand out, my mentor then encouraged me to focus on female entrepreneurs. A spark in me aligned with this idea because my **why** is giving a voice to others, making one feel visible when they have felt lost. I would be telling their brand story through my pictures, so they felt heard and understood. I photographed my clients in the most beautiful, authentic way I possibly could. *Wow! Why hadn't I thought of this before?* Photographing entrepreneurs was the perfect direction to add to my work.

By working with entrepreneurs, I was able to see how empowering branding shoots were. A personal branding shoot takes a person and gives their message a voice. It brings their vision to life as something tangible. And once they had a voice, these women were invincible. Helping women project their message gives me so much joy.

I have since photographed many wonderful women.

My Roots

I am so blessed to be able to do what I love, and I didn't think this could be possible for me. I was brought up to believe academia was the only route worth perusing.

I grew up on a council estate in Birmingham, England, in the '70s and '80s. My father had come to the UK to follow his passion for doing a PhD in the UK. He was a scientist, and he desired to get a British degree. I was the eldest of four children with three younger brothers. As my father was a student for much of my childhood, my mother worked to make ends meet. A working mother and a father who was studying meant that I had to step up and look after my brothers from a very young age. From as young as seven, I took on the responsibilities of getting myself and my brothers off to school every morning and tidy up the house before my mum returned from a busy day at work. It sounds harsh, but I didn't know any different.

I had an eclectic upbringing. I grew up on a mostly racist council estate, which crushed my self-worth. But I managed to muddle through this by finding a small group of friends that accepted me for me. I had friends that were local to the estate but also had family friends that were doctors and lawyers. This taught me to be able to talk to all people from all walks of life. I could chat with the locals on the estate as well as prominent CEOs and people of power with confidence.

I'm very grateful for this journey because although it was tough when I look back, it taught me some fundamental lessons.

It taught me that people are people, and we must be kind and respect one another.

It taught me resilience. Despite it being a racist environment, as long as I restricted myself to certain people, I could minimise the effect on me.

It taught me branding from a young age. Stick to your values, and you will attract your tribe. Not all the people on the estate were racist. Your value doesn't decrease by someone else's inability to see your worth! I had to align myself with people who accepted me.

Lastly, it taught me how to visualise. Despite my challenges academically, I always imagined myself in a better situation, and that life was going to be better. I did get to university, something my teachers didn't think was possible for me. Visualisation, coupled with action, works! I honestly don't think I would be where I am now without these experiences.

The Wisdom and Lessons Learned

Having travelled this journey to success, I list below the key lessons I've learned on the way. I hope that you'll find strength from my wisdom because you're **worthy** of success too!

#1 Have Your Voice

The wisdom I have learnt from my experience is there is something empowering about having a voice. Especially if it's your voice echoing your values. There is something freeing about being heard. Find a way in which you can put your emotions into something that helps you feel visible and heard. Being authentic and having your message heard and understood is how to step into your **power**. You won't step into your power by trying to be like others. That's when your message becomes lost amongst the sea of sameness, and that's when you lose you. If my values and my personal experience did not clearly define my brand, then I may never have been seen or chosen by Lily Pebbles. There are thousands of photographers out there, but she chose me!

#2 Investing in Your Brand

If you are in business or thinking of starting a business, then investing in your brand is a must! If you want to get high-ticket clients, you have to think big. People choose **you** because of the promise you have made in your brand. What is your promise? My promise is beautiful, authentic, storytelling images full of emotion, light, and connection. When someone chooses to book me, they know what they are getting. They have already brought into my brand and my promise. Investing in your brand is the best investment you can do because it aligns you to your ideal client. Done correctly, your brand does all the selling for you.

#3 A Big Why

Your '**why**' has to be bigger than your fear! This is a big one. The thing is I didn't want to create generic images of women holding coffee cups sitting by a computer. I wanted to capture these women authentically. I wanted to capture their '**why**', their personality, their personal stamp of uniqueness. I wanted to capture their soul and tell their story. It had to shine through in my images. I had to give these women a voice because I knew how it saved me and propelled me forward. So, my '**why**' was now bigger than my fear.

#4 What You Focus on Expands

Stop focusing on what you think you are <u>not,</u> and start focusing on what you can become. See the result. Visualise it until it becomes real in your head and then do it. I found by seeing it first in my mind's eye made it possible! It helped me <u>feel</u> that it could be possible. The truth is 'anything' I have ever visualised has always materialised. It's so important to focus on the thing you want to achieve and <u>not</u> your fear. If I had focused on the negative, then I wouldn't have been able to work through my blocks. The way forward is to focus on the positive. What you focus on becomes your reality!

The Reward

I am so grateful for the brand I have created. I have continued to photograph some amazing women from powerful CEOs of companies to high-profile influencers and coaches. I have been invited to be interviewed on *TedEd* and *Podcasts*. My photographs have been published in high-profile magazines and mainstream newspapers. I've become a best-selling author. I love empowering women with a voice and spreading their message.

Let go of your fear by focusing on the outcome you want in your life and don't overthink things. Like the brand Nike said in one of their campaigns,
'Just do it'!
Success Actions
Here are four things you can do right now.

1. Define your 'why'. It has to move you. It has to be bigger than your fear.
2. Write down your goal – your big dream.
3. Visualise it!
4. Do one thing today that will move you closer to your goal. Don't overthink it!

'Be humble. Not knowing something does not make you a fraud, it makes you a student!'
~ Maria Forleo.

You've got this!

Much love,

Razia xx

About the Author

Razia Naqvi-Jukes is a personal brand photographer, filmmaker, and consultant. She lives in London, UK, with her husband and three children.

She loves helping women define their brand and help project its message. Her methods have helped elevate her brand and the brand of others. She has worked with famous influencers and entrepreneurs. She is a best-selling author of *She Made It Happen* and has been featured in *TedEd*: The Impact of your images on social media.

Contacts

Join My Free Mini-course: The Art of The Six Figure Brand Accelerator.
https://www.facebook.com/groups/692877941444939

Website: https://razia.photography/personal-brand-photographer

Instagram: https://www.instagram.com/raziajukesphoto/

Facebook: https://www.facebook.com/razia.naqvijukes/

Linkedin: https://www.linkedin.com/in/razia-naqvi-jukes-5037631b0/

TedEd: The Impact of Your Images on Social Media
https://ed.ted.com/on/GoBIIdsY?fbclid=IwAR234UkPjJIrwXLDztPIIPVpFmK
dHjgtjgIAGdW3YyAOQVTwo9SZsJLkwPs

Undergoing the Transformation from Earning to Receiving

Release Ab-Use and Start Receiving Money Aligned with You!

Tammy Ketura Mock-Andrejowich
Peace Expert and Fate Transformation Specialist, Switzerland

'I receive pain as gold nuggets, with joy and gratitude.'

~ Tammy Ketura Mock-Andrejowich

The Meltdown

'Tammy, I wanted to inform you personally that you did not get the job.' Racing forward, he continued, 'There were so many exceptional candidates, …' It was the 28th of September 2018. His words rang in my ears. Like a glowing fire poker, they pierced my soul with a sizzle. Tears swelled my eyes, burned wet trails down my cheeks, and landed with one solemn splash, dazzling the naked oak table with sudden brightness. Then again, with waging finger, he continued, 'Tammy, you will **never** earn an income with The Work'.

I was in shock! He vehemently expressed the worst I believed could happen to me, It was as if, with each wag, his finger pushed the curse into my reality.

The Turning Point

It was time for me to face reality. Ever since I moved to Switzerland in 2008, straight after getting my Master's in Arts degree, I was behind the employment eight-ball! My excellent academic and extracurricular profile was discredited because my German was a second language, and I held foreign diplomas. Out of necessity, I started working in a few restaurants, constantly hoping that something in my line of expertise would open up. Eventually, we started our own restaurant. And then when I left my marital relationship, I left my place of employment, the social network that supported me since I arrived in Switzerland, and my home. I was alone with our daughter in Switzerland. One thing was certain – I would never work in a restaurant again.

Immediately after I left the restaurant in August 2012, our family doctor decided I needed three months of sick leave. Life was chaos. At first, my daughter and I lived at a friend's parent's place until I got my social assistance and unemployment insurance in order, and then we moved into our own apartment. In reality, I was unable to work long after those three months had passed. The gaslighting was so intense, it was internalised in my body and literally immobilised me. The accusations, criticisms, and belittling I experienced in my previous relationship were so alive in my mind that any decision I had to make sent my body-mind into that pattern of 'having to prevent something', 'having to make something happen', 'having to avoid something'. I was caught in flashback after flashback and trauma after trauma.

A collection of professionals were supporting me to de-escalate the situation. My body showed the typical signs of CPTSD and anxiety: insomnia, inability to self-soothe, high cortisol levels, exhausted adrenal glands, lack of appetite, digestive problems, unable to fall asleep, incapacity to focus, and to top it off, I was constantly intimidated by myself. Internalised violence acts like an auto-immune disease, and our egos' survival strategy begins to self-attack. My approval-seeking was killing me.

I spent years healing my mind, my body, and cleaning up the systems pulling me down. I was fed up with people finding reasons not to hire me rather than to hire me. I noticed their complaints about my profile had everything to do with them and nothing to do with my work ethic, tenacity, intelligence, capacity, or the value I could bring to a given situation. Interestingly, in Canada, no matter what I put my heart into, it succeeded with flying colours! It was time to rise above the locally generated limitations and without leaving my office, create a business that supported my daughter, and allow me to live my dream.

The Impact

When I got home, I cried my despair out, then I did what I love to do: I served myself peace and freedom on demand, with reliability, and independent from everything else. I got still, listened, and this is what showed up inside my mind's eye.

> *I am irate at him because he is cursing me.*
> *I want him to support me.*
> *He should see how his support is invaluable for my success.*
> *I need him to blaze my trail.*
> *He is confused, hurtful, shocking, violating, afraid of reality.*
> *I do not ever want him to violate my integrity again.*
> ~ The Judge-Your-Neighbour-Worksheet, The
> Work of Byron Katie, thework.com, © 2020

After I was done writing, I inquired into each statement with *The Work.* I witnessed as each statements' turnarounds and examples showed up. I saw how it was truer that **I** was cursing **me**. The images of all the times I poured out my heart, applied, and did not get the job, rushed through my mind stuck on repeat. My mind picked them up as proof that in the future, this would reoccur continuously. I witnessed, he was not cursing me, he was talking out of his worst-case scenarios for himself, and I wanted **me** to support **me**!

It was only I who saw myself during the late nights, the early mornings, and the effort I put into landing a permanent position. I want me to support me with gentleness, with patience and space, with direction, give my vision legs, and permission, so that even without proof, I can confidently experience successes now, and succeed in the future. I should see how my support is invaluable for my success. This means that when I feel scared, depressed, stuck, or set a timeline that is unrealistic for me, I care for me and support me out of discomfort and back into now that supports me growing a company, living a health lifestyle, and speaking supportively towards myself and my accomplishments. Self-realisation provided clarity and empowered.

Then, I leaned into his curse and received its innate blessings. 'Tammy, you will **always** earn an income with The Work,' because, **I** hire **me**. I choose how I to spend my time, what value I bring, what method I work with, and what service I provide! The 'Poor me. I will never earn a permanent position in Switzerland', became 'Yahoo!! I will never earn a permanent position in Switzerland!'

I leaned into why this is the best thing that could ever happen to me! I fell in love with myself again. My story left me, new capacities flowed out of me, connection reigned. I was back in my state of happiness, openness, and being loved. Instructions followed. I scrapped my last pennies together and purchased a course on 'how to grow a consulting business'.

Life had something else cut out for me.

The Truth Will Set You Free

Feet walk, the heart pumps, lungs breath, and our mind produce images. These images are always changing. When an image, also named a 'thought', gets stuck. That is named 'trauma'. Trauma is a stuck thought. We do not need to have experienced a traumatising or dramatic situation for a thought to get stuck. When a thought is stuck, my mind can prod it into existence, and my actions follow in a limited way – to prevent, avoid, or make it happen. This shows up in my thinking, feeling, acting, and what we experience in our world, and this is the order of creation. My interaction feels unnatural, and inside, my body feels rough.

Although I had completed my relationship clean up work before I started my business, it was humbling to notice how images of the past showed up and were acting as proof and begging for intimacy again. For example, the thought 'I am not enough' provided what seemed like a plethora of proof. Trying to force it out of my mind felt violent. Alternatively, when I got still, the thoughts had to do with a few specific images of the past, such as where my first husband expressed his judgments about me. This image was connected to other thoughts like *I need an authority figure to approve of me*, *I am not enough to give myself permission*, and *I need an institution to hold my back*. I noticed that these thought systems were devouring my time and mental space. I was determined to 'get productive'. At that time, I believed that meant stop spending this time on cleaning up my mind. Then, I realised that caring and opening up my mind provided for flow and clarity towards myself, clients, and my business. I then made it a priority to include this practice in my daily business matters. So, when I was feeling stuck, confused, trapped, etc., instead, of mentally bulling, beating, manipulating, or violating myself into action, I had a choice. My alternative was to get still, be listened to, write the stressful thoughts down, inquire into them, be witnessed, and experience their turnarounds. Even on this level, violence left me and abundance flowed in.

The effects on daily life and business operations were phenomenal. There was enough time in the day to play with my daughter, cook, and grow my business. There was enough money to pay for business applications and cover our monthly expenses. My mind and body provided for so much space, I smoothly learn how to create a website, reach out to potential clients, conduct strategy sessions, and receive 'nos' with empowerment and without an emotional hangover. Instructions that I receive are enough to put in action. Caring for me is caring for my business, and the realisations continued. I am my business! This means that caring for my fears opened me up to a world of abundance that was happening **for** me! This habit keeps my nervous system smooth, receiving, and consistently opens my mind, my body, my actions, my life, and my business to new capacities. It grew the big fat success that my life and business enjoy and benefit from.

The Ordinary World

One of the many things I love about thinking is that an 'old' reoccurring thought, experienced in a 'new' context, is actually, in essence, a new thought. Just recently, I noticed 'not enough' creep back into my life with their former fervour and fear to be seen. This time the thought was connected with lead generation, *I am not finding enough of the **right** people*. When I got still, I witnesses my security dependent on the leads I was generating. I noticed how I went to bed much later than I desired with the effort to 'compensate' the dissatisfaction. I woke up much later than desired because I worked too late into the night. My day started out uncomfortably and without the usual morning satisfaction. To catch up with the day for sleeping in late, I would skip out on my morning yoga routine. Out of 'not enough' work done before I go to lunch, I would postpone my lunch and then argue myself out of it, with the aspiration of 'motivating' myself to get 'enough' work done and to 'earn' lunch. And the cycle continued. When I inquired into this thought, my world shifted: I woke up satisfied, took a two-hour lunch break, took the time to go outside, move my body, and be tantalised by the elements. I would eat delicious food and take the time to really taste it and enjoy it. I would go to bed on time and satisfied. I woke up satisfied and focused. My quality of my work incredibly increased. Stressless and filled with joy, I loved the shifts my life received again.

Daily life is the experience and celebration that I am enough. I do not need an institution to provide me with authority. I am that authority, and I provide myself with permission. When any thought gets in the way of that, or some motive blocks me, I clean it up kindly and succinctly. I **choose** me. **Only** I can choose me. **Only** I can take me seriously. This is my innate job to share my gifts in the world without propitiating an experience of lack.

Today, I own a business that I am deeply proud of. I receive my fears, blockages, stuck-ness, and trapped-ness, as a gift. Instead of exerting any form of violence, like 'should-ing' myself or others, negative judgements, or force something into/out existence, and I receive money in alignment with my true nature. I am constantly aligning with my heart, from messaging, approaching new clients through to delivering services. The services are reliable and provide shifts beyond the mind's imagination. I daily support others to align with themselves. Everything is happening **for** me, and not **to** me!

I host a beautiful online course portal with modules and incredible bonuses, which includes step-by-step video training and documents to download. I work with fantastic people that I love. Our weekly live question and answer and deep-dive inquiry sessions are touching and inspiring. Our support, accountability, insights, realisations group, and live mentorship, are genuine, and self-realisation based. And most generously, the shifts come smoothly, gently, are integrated in life, and grow our independence. After we do *The Work*, the work keeps working. I invite you to partake in my **free** 3-Day Accelerator course where you can experience your own undoing and receive your shifts.

> **Yes!** To Myself!! Stop Abuse – Start Abundance
> *(As I align, the name for this product may change.)*
> https://tammymock.clickfunnels.com/program-registration

> **Yes!** To Myself! **Money!!** Stop AB-Use – Start Alignment
> *(As I align, the name for this product may change.)*
> https://tammymock.clickfunnels.com/program-registration-yes-to-myself-money

Key Lessons and Words of Wisdom

Here are lessons I learned. The self-realisation they provided for me and my life shifted me from limiting understandings from 'I need to earn money' to abundant mindsets of 'I receive money'. I invite you to let each one speak to you.

1. **Experiencing Freedom and Security Is Independent of the Future**

   Images of the future are not proof nor security. 'This month, I need to earn…!' 'My goal is…' 'When I get this … done, then…' What I love about earning money, and the only thing I am control of is, now. The future doesn't exist. 'I am a conduit. The future shows me why the money comes in. It is backwards'. (Byron Katie, *Question Your Thinking, Change Your World'*).

2.   Choosing Action over Perfection

There are so many new skills to learn, and so many tasks to accomplish, and so many decisions that I was confronted with for the first time, I began to notice how my desire to 'do it right' or 'make it perfect' completely disabled me to take action. Then I started giving myself permission not to be perfect and to choose 'learning by doing'. My workflow processes relaxed. I was able to move with more ease through the complicated website-building and enjoy it!

Perfection comes from the time spent tweaking, not the time spent on the product behind closed doors. And that tweaking grows out of the relationship responding to new, reoccurring, and potential clients' needs.

3.   Wanting Is Scary

The longer I dance around what I want, the harder it is to be the authority in my life and what my business needs. The harder it is to make decisions intuitively and receive their results with excitement. My intimidations about what I wanted prevented me and my company from growing naturally. Take these seriously. Being aligned with my wants and experiencing the freedom that I have everything in any given moment, that is there is nothing to loose, has been a beautiful combo in my life receiving and giving, that is growing, with ease and flow.

4.   Being Motivated Is Often Celebrated as a Great Characteristic

It can also be a phenomenal blocker. When I experience motivation, in my mind's eye, there is a lot for me to lose. This fear of losing something is the perfect blocker. Losing this fear of losing, opens me to receive. This is the trick with earning money and a lot of freedom!

5.   Keeping the Nervous System Calm, Keeps Me Receiving

How many opportunities did I receive because my nervous system was calm? Every single one! Each opportunity I said '**<u>yes!</u>**' to, provided positive shifts in me and my business. And I did not receive the opportunity because I felt that had extra money or had spare time, and I did accept the opportunity because I had the capacity. I was able to integrate every opportunity with grace and eagerness, and never with an emotional hangover attacking myself that I was 'wasting money' or 'purchasing something that was not needed'. A calm nervous system supports a natural growth of capacity. What methods do you know to bring you home, **independent** of the situation, again, and again? In my programs, I use *The Work of Byron Katie* because it is simple, reliable, efficient, grows independence, and we get to laugh a lot!

6. **Being Honest with Myself Includes My Physical Sensations**

I often hear clients say that being honest requires courage. To get the results I enjoy, being honest with myself is a must. The institution my business creates relies on it. Honesty is connected to adding value; adding value is connected to providing a service; providing a service is connected to leadership; leadership depends on honesty. This quality of transparency provides space for vulnerability, authenticity, and integrity. Embodying these qualities attracts people to me and to trust my services.

7. **Being Generous with Timelines**

I am my timeline. Timelines affect my satisfaction and empowerment in my life. In the beginning, when learning all these new skills, my timelines were completely off. I had absolutely no track record of how long something would take me. I constantly felt like life was against me every time I did not reach a timeline. This habit was wearing me down. I needed to stop that mental habit of feeling like a failure. I started to be generous with me and my timelines. I hook onto my goals, then I let go of them and follow my instructions. They make me and move me, and before I even realise it, my goals have already been reached! Life is fun and growing my business too!!

8. **'YES!' To myself is exhilarating!**

When I needed a new skillset or approach, there was a brilliant person waiting around the corner for me. This means me backing my desires all the way.

The Rewards

It is rewarding to have transformed the first uncertainties of growing a business into living in freedom and security! I'm growing my business to six figures and I en-**joy** every moment of it. I have been featured in the media, invited as an expert to public talks, been published as a #1 International Best Selling Author. I offer two exceptional programs that support people to daily experience life as everything is happening **for** you, and not **to** you! At the moment, I am working on my solo book; *Get Still: Gain Peace and Confidence and Shed Narcissistic, Co-Dependent, Toxic, and Love-Addictive Relationships from the Inside Out*. And I am spearheading a multi-author project featuring 20 professionals supporting people who have healed from narcissistic abuse, named *I AM: Releasing the Shame of Narcissistic Abuse and Transforming Financial Abuse to Wealth Beyond Numbers,* release December 2020. Excitingly, most recently I have been interviewed by *TED-Ed* titled: `How My Abuse Transformed Me to a Lover of What Is`.

'Give yourself permission to give yourself permission!'
~ Tammy Ketura Mock-Andrejowich

Powerful Summary

Let's recap the powerful points from this chapter.
1. Self-blame, self-criticism, self-accusation, self-sabotage, self-manipulation, arguing with what is, and motives, etc., create a hostile environment towards life and consume space that blocks creativity, business growth, and receiving money.

2. My clients, my business, and myself are worth every moment in time and money I spend on cleaning these up.

3. Alignment feels like bliss. When I diligently care for my realm of responsibility, joy makes me unstoppable.

Success Actions

Implement these actions to support your daily success:

1. Notice sensations of blockages, stuck-ness, shame, motivations, and trapped-ness.

2. Gently and thoroughly clean up what irritates and hurts in the inner world. Opening ourselves up to receiving starts with receiving our own inner world.

3. Give yourself permission to give yourself permission!

'You are the Queen that you have been waiting for!'
~ Tammy Ketura Mock-Andrejowich

In adoration to you and you on your journey,

Xo Tammy September 19th, 2020

Tammy Ketura Mock-Andrejowich

About the Author

Tammy Ketura Mock-Andrejowich's affinity for peace and freedom started as a small child. In elementary, Tammy eagerly joined the 'peace-makers' program for the playground hours. She completed her Bachelor of Arts Honours in Sociology and Conflict resolution from the University of Winnipeg and from Menno Simons College. She earned her Masters of Arts in Costa Rica from the United Nations-mandated University for Peace. Desiring to leave the theoretics of the academy, she completed her MA thesis in Haiti.

Interestingly, her desire to understand the crux of violence found her, not on a UN Peacekeeping Mission, but rather in the lush emerald slopes of Switzerland. Taking the risk, she set her vision high, that is to transform her fate from the inside out. Leaving no rock unturned, she unraveled the riddle of violence, trauma, stress, being stuck, and being trapped, from the inside out. Now she receives life from the position where everything is happening **for** her, and not **to** her. She left suffering behind and is now empowering others to end their suffering.

She and her daughter love biking around, hiking to the mountain tops, swimming in the pristine waters, and painting outside.

'Ketura' is Hebrew and means to 'transform into the rising up of sweet-smelling fragrance'.

Contacts

Website: www.keturaconsulting.com

Email: tammy@keturaconsulting.com

Facebook: https://www.facebook.com/tammy.mockandrejowich

LinkedIn: https://www.linkedin.com/in/tammy-ketura-mock-andrejowich-b310a316b/

Youtube:
https://www.youtube.com/channel/UCEgQvTU07CeyYHmorFvWuTQ/featured?disable_polymer=1

Twitter: https://twitter.com/TammyKMockAndre

Instagram: https://www.instagram.com/tammyketuramockandrejowich/

Books:

Mock-Andrejowich, T. K. (2019). Tammy Ketura Mock-Andrejowich. In *Change Makers: 20 Transformational Stories from Women Making an Impact in the Lives of Others.* Change Makers Press.

I AM: Releasing the Shame of Narcissistic Abuse and Transforming Financial Abuse to Wealth Beyond Numbers. The story of 20 professionals serving people on their journeys out of financial abuse and into abundance. Release December 2020

Get Still: Gain Peace and Confidence and Shed Narcissistic, Co-Dependent, Toxic, and Love-Addictive Relationships from the Inside Out, being written

Ted ED Interview: 'How My Abuse Transformed Me to a Lover of What Is'
https://ed.ted.com/on/Hf8lAWCT

Consistency Is Key

Vandee Flake
Elite Network Marketer and Entrepreneur, USA

*"You will never change your life until you change
something you do daily.
The secret of your success is found in your daily
routine."*
~ John C Maxwell

The morning I took the pregnancy test, I was ecstatic. My life was moving right along the track I had planned out in high school. I had graduated top of my class and earned a scholarship. After graduation, I had a job that paid well, and I had moved up to a manager position. My husband and I had one darling little girl and were trying for our baby number two. My husband, Sam, was working as a teacher, and we had just remodeled our home. However, the top-of-the-world feeling didn't last. One morning I woke up, bleeding. I called my doctor and went in to hear the devastating news that I had miscarried our sweet baby. Not knowing what else to do, I went to work as normal. I didn't tell my boss for a week.

Why do we, as women, push ourselves so hard to be perfect at everything? Why did I feel the stress of my job was more important than my health and my family? I realized that I had given up on my goal to work from home so I could balance my work and family.

We were able to have another baby. The pregnancy was rough, and I knew that I could not do it again and work the stressful job that I had. We had been living in a rut with work and two kids. We were not putting our marriage on our priority list, and we were barely surviving.

Becoming an Entrepreneur

It was during this overwhelming time in our life when my husband informed me that a friend invited us to a network marketing meeting. I reluctantly agreed to go but told my husband he was not to bring his wallet or credit card. Quickly, I realized that this wasn't a me-too product, and I was intrigued by the story and the science behind this. I did realize the possibilities, but I didn't let the slick-talking, out-of-town friend blow the opportunity out of proportion. After a rather quick study of the company and the science, Sam went to meet with the leaders. Finally, we decided to dip our toe in.

Now, one thing that I really dislike about the network marketing industry is false expectations are usually set. If you want to make the income of a doctor or lawyer, you know how much time and schooling that takes. If you want to be successful in any industry, you need to invest an average of 10,000 hours. However, most people are content with the 40:50 plan – work 40 hours a week, for 40 to 50 years, then retire on 40% of your paycheck. The brilliant part of network marketing, in my opinion, is the opportunity to learn from millionaires and billionaires on the techniques and strategies that they used to get to where they are. The education portion is equal to the action. The other amazing thing in this industry is you can earn while you learn. As you polish your skills, you become a better version of yourself.

You Become the Sum of the Five People You Spend the Most Time With

At my first big event, I remember a speaker sharing that you become the sum of the five people you spend the most time with. Never had a quote hit my soul with more force, and I love quotes. I sat pondering for days because I realized that, with the exception of Sam, the other four people were co-workers, who I did not want to become. I had become a version of Vandee that was worried about work, did not put in her best effort, and did not reach for her goals or dreams anymore. I had become complacent and apathetic. I feel like apathy is one of the hardest things that I struggle with. It is so easy to become distracted from our dreams and let apathy lead the way. You become the average of the five people you spend the most time with. **<u>Pick wisely!</u>** You choose who you listen to and learn from.

Pick wise mentors. Read or listen to authors to help you become the best version of yourself.

This realization that I was meant to do more than go to work and die, that I needed to become the best version of me that I could be, was hard to take. Realizing you are apathetic and living in a rut is a hard slap in the face. So, I began a two-pronged approach; I did two things every day.

I learned something new. Some days it was the same CD over and over again. There are so many amazing resources that you can use for personal growth. A few of my favorites include John Maxwell, Bob Proctor, Mel Robbins, Eric Worre, and many other personal development coaches.

The second was I took action.

Daily Activity

John Maxwell speaks about the importance of taking time every day to work towards your goals. He states that every day he reads, writes. and edits. People ask him, "But John, what about Christmas or your birthday?"

He responds, "Every day, I read, write, and reflect – not all day, but a little bit every day."

There is such power in daily, consistent action. Whether it is building as an entrepreneur or writing a book, daily activity consistently, over time, will have amazing results. Look at John Maxwell, he is a legend with over 25 best-selling self-help books. His courses are amazing and inspiring.

This action of daily activity wasn't easy. The simple little steps were easy to do, and they were easy to skip. It wasn't an "Ah-ha!", brilliant moment that you do once, and your life changes forever. It was the little, almost invisible, steps forward that accumulated to cause a huge change in our life.

I struggled with learning something new every day. I was busy. I worked a full-time job, often skipping breaks and lunches for work. I had two small children, and we were active in the community and our church. So, I decided that I would enroll in a mobile university. My driving time (one hour each day) became my classroom. I listened to recorded calls, bought CDs, and listened to them over and over. I remember a training where the millionaire said, "I can't sit in your car each day and motivate you." I thought, *Man, I wish he could!*

The first CD I bought was a recording of that exact speaker. I thought, *I have this now. I can have any trainer I want with me all the time.* Where can you squeeze in your learning? What about the shower or the car in the early morning? You can do it!

Decide your daily routine and schedule these training sessions into your day. If it's working out, make calls, learn more about your business, or work with clients. **<u>Schedule it!</u>**

I try to focus on four core areas of my life each day: social, mental, physical, and spiritual. One little step each day will make a huge difference. I have found that I achieve my goals faster when I put it on my calendar with a reminder. I have a bad habit of not wanting to write down little things or schedule things that don't take long, but when it's on my calendar, I realize that I do better.

Write Down Your Goals

The next inspiration that hit me right between the eyes was a learning session on goals. I felt like I didn't have any goals left. However, there was one goal that I had discarded as unattainable and unrealistic. Sitting in that class woke that goal up and brought it to the forefront of my mind and heart. I wanted to be an entrepreneur so I could work from home and raise my babies. I also decided that my "momma heart" had been cheated, and I wanted a third baby that I could raise.

My goal to have flexibility and time choice soon became the forefront of my daily activity. Number one, I had the desire. Number two, I wrote it everywhere. Funny story about this, I came home at midnight from this training, cleaned off the mirror in my room, and wrote four goals down:

1.   Mom home from work

2.   Baby #3

3. $10,000 checks

4.   Debt Free

My daughter came in the next morning, and with her little hand on her hip, she reminded me of the rule to only draw on paper, not the mirror. We had a quick discussion on goals, and why we write our goals where we can see them. She asked if we could add Disneyland to the list. So, #5 became "Disneyland for the family" goal.

Daily Action Pays Off

After 30 months of focused learning and activity, we reached a point where we could make a change in our lives. I retired from my job the next Monday, and I found out that my goal of having our third child was coming true also. However, with the completion of this huge goal, we were able to make family time a priority. We were financially blessed to have options.

Our business expanded again with a wonderful team in Hawaii. I flew over there seven months pregnant to meet with an incredible tribe. The one thing that I didn't realize up to this point in my entrepreneurial business was the health and financial benefits were amazing, but the **friendships that have been created will change you into a better version of yourself.**

This business has introduced me to friends all over the world, people I would have never met if I hadn't become an entrepreneur! Daily action will pay off. The creation of this lifestyle did not happen immediately. Instead, it was a compound effect of daily activity.

Take Time to Rest, not Quit

After my son was born, I dived back into traveling and building my business. My adorable sidekick traveled to eleven different states, including Florida and Hawaii, before he was a year old. I created a network of women who wanted options to travel and the choice on how to raise their families. My life was incredibly blessed. Our business had doubled in size, and life was fun.

I went to an all-women's event, and I came home so excited and so sick. Everyone at the event ended up with a cold, so I didn't think much about being sick. My husband flew out to work with a team across the country, and I didn't get better. I found out that I was pregnant again. This was a high-risk pregnancy because of medical complications. I was in constant fear of losing the baby. I also had a toddler who needed me and two older children in school. We had just purchased a small pizza business that we were trying to get up and running.

In the midst of all this stress, I heard this quote, "Take time to rest, but don't quit." Sam and I re-evaluated our priorities and closed the pizza shop. We canceled travel plans and put the family as a top priority. We hired help to get through the tasks that were too overwhelming. We took the time we needed. We rested, but we did not quit. After my sweet boy was born, healthy and strong, I had to have two surgeries the next year. However, we took time to enjoy our sweet baby. When life gets overwhelming, it's okay to take time to rest, but don't quit. Don't give up on your dreams and goals because it gets hard.

Life is an Adventure – Vision Boards

On our vision board, we added several more goals: a cute little farm, travel, and adventures as a family. After our baby was born, we bought a little farm out of town. We raised cows, pigs, sheep, dogs, cats, and chickens. This presented good lessons for our kids to learn responsibility and work ethic. We also learned about keeping animals safe from hawks, crows, and coyotes. We had some sad days and some great memories. About the time that we had the little farm all situated, Sam decided it was time to move again. I was devastated for a bit, but we discussed our goals and dreams, and decided to be crazy.

We sold everything and bought an RV. We left Arizona and headed East. We realized a few things early on. Traveling full time is not like a vacation. You have to plan downtime for work, laundry, walks, school, and just to chill. After slowing down our travels, we had some incredible and crazy adventures. We enjoyed seeing friends and new places. The memories we created will last forever. We also enjoyed exploring historical sites with our kids. I could write a book just on the lessons we learned and the places we saw. We flew to Cancun for 11 days in February of 2020, and the adventure was truly memorable. We decided when we got home that we might extend our 18-month RV trip and looked at international destinations. Sam and I had traveled to Europe, the Bahamas, and Mexico, but we wanted to experience this with our children.

However, the next month, all plans were changed as COVID-19 hit. Living in an RV with four children when you couldn't even go to a playground was scary. As plans were canceled and life was changing, we re-evaluated our goals. It was curious to me that with all the beautiful places we had seen in our travels, our kids wanted to go home to be closer to family and friends. We were able to buy a home, and we are settling back into a routine. Every decision needs to be evaluated to determine if it will bring us closer to our goals or if it is just a distraction.

Three Steps to Get Back on Track

Becoming the best version of yourself is not a one time, aha! moment. It is the small daily actions that compound to change your life. "When life hits you, and you feel like staying in bed under the covers, curled up in the fetal position. What do you do?"

I've been there many times in my journey. One of my dear friends and mentors, Seth Mulder, who created the concept of CEO, *Creating Entrepreneurs Online*, shared this, and it felt like the perfect thing to share with you. Here are three steps to get you back on track.

First, stop and count your blessings. Don't just say "I'm grateful." Really stop to count the blessings you have in your life. List them out, name them one by one. I try to add three blessings to my gratitude chart every day. When I hit the down times, I realized that I have usually slacked off in my gratitude list.

The second step is to reconnect to your vision. What's your vision, and why do you want to succeed? Reconnect to your vision. I highly recommend a vision board or goal sheet somewhere visible that you'll see every day.

The third step is to take action. Action each day creates a compound effect that will change your life.

Apathy vs. Happiness

I've realized that happiness is a choice. We cannot control everything that happens to us, but we can control how we react. I've found a few things that help me find daily happiness. These little things each day will make a big difference: gratitude, outside time, exercise, sleep, drinking enough water, and eating right. Then add your daily activity to achieve your visions and goals. These ways are how you choose happiness.

Being an entrepreneur is a daily battle against naysayers and your own insecurities. However, daily activity will change your life.

Yes, I can do it, and **yes, you can also.**

Power Summary

1. You become the average of the five people you spend the most time with. **Pick wisely!**

2. Decide your daily routine and schedule them into your day.

3. Be specific on your gratitude list and your goals.

Success Actions

1. Spend at least 15 minutes a day with one of your mentors. Learn and grow every single day.

2. Take time each day for you to visualize your goals. Take a walk, meditate, but think about your goals.

3. Spend time working for your goals. Decide what action needs taken every single day and schedule it into your calendar.

Live with intention. Walk to the edge. Listen hard. Practice wellness. Play with abandon. Laugh. Choose with no regret. Do what you love. Live as if this is all there is."

Vandee Flake

~ Mary Anne Roadacher-Hershey

Best wishes.

Vandee Flake

About the Author

Vandee Flake is a native Arizonian. She graduated from Arizona State University in 2003, followed by a nine-year career in marketing. However, once she became a mom, she realized that this wasn't the career path that would give her the time flexibility to be a modern-day mother.

Vandee and her husband started their journey ten years ago in network marketing. This has been the answer to their prayers for better health and more time flexibility for their family. Vandee is passionate about helping entrepreneurs and encouraging women live their own dreams. She has built a successful business and loves to help others.

Vandee and her family traveled full time in an RV with their children for 18 months. This may have been the best or the craziest decision for them. COVID-19 has changed their plans for now.

Vandee's goal is to connect with other people who are looking for better health, finances, or more time freedom for themselves and their families.

Contacts

Instagram: www.instagram.com/travelingflakes

Facebook (Business): www.facebook.com/happinessjellybeans

Facebook (Personal): https://www.facebook.com/vandee.flake

Email: vflake@gmail.com